"For many of us, the world's problems just seem too big and too hard to face. It's so much easier for us to retreat from them than to take them on. *Relentless* offers raw inspiration and biblical application that empowers Christians to participate in the spiritual and physical transformation of their world. This book emanates out of the personal experiences of Dave Donaldson and Convoy of Hope, who have served nobly in mobilizing hundreds of thousands of people to distribute vast amounts of resources and live out the whole gospel of Jesus Christ among the poor and suffering."

—RICH STEARNS
President of World Vision US
and author of *The Hole in Our Gospel*

"This book is a clear biblical call for compassion for the poor. Dave Donaldson provides practical guidance and a powerful witness to the transformation God brings about in everyone involved when we join the compassion revolution."

—JONATHAN T. M. RECKFORD
CEO, Habitat for Humanity International

"The convoy of compassionate groups is growing, and Dave Donaldson is playing a prominent role. *Relentless* shows that relational justice—people helping others, one-to-one—is the key to developing social justice."

—MARVIN OLASKY
Editor-in-chief, *World* magazine
Former provost, The King's College, NYC

"*Relentless* challenges readers to serve the poor and suffering in America and around the world. I have seen Convoy of Hope grow to help millions by providing them with food, clean water, and shelter. It has truly been a catalyst for meeting physical and spiritual needs."

—DR. GEORGE O. WOOD
General Superintendent, Assemblies of God

"The cross is both vertical and horizontal. It leads to salvation and transformation, covenant and community, John 3:16 and Matthew 25. In *Relentless,* Dave Donaldson reconciles the vertical and horizontal elements of the Christian message, mobilizing a movement of hope that will feed the hungry in both body and soul. Let the revolution begin!"

—SAMUEL RODRÍGUEZ
President, National Hispanic Christian Leadership Conference

"This book will give you an insider's look at compassion ministry and turn your world upside down—or maybe I should say, right side up."

—MARK BATTERSON
Pastor National Community Church, Washington, D.C.
Best-Selling Author

"*Relentless* is a passionate and persuasive book that will move you to tears, cause you to laugh, and inspire you to make a difference."

—ANNE BEILER
Founder of Auntie Anne's Pretzels

"A must read for Christians worldwide. These are the issues we must confront. And this is the legacy of hope we must leave. And all written by a man who has overcome extraordinary challenges to make an extraordinary impact on the world."

—Doug Wead
Former Senior Advisor for Presidents
George H. W. Bush and George W. Bush

"Dave Donaldson's life is a testament to the transforming force of Christian love and compassion. He loves because he was loved first; he shows compassion because it was first shown to him. *Relentless* tells the story of the power of the gospel that must be good news to the poor and freedom for the oppressed."

—Jim Wallis
President of Sojourners
Author of *The Great Awakening* and *On God's Side*

RELENTLESS

PURSUING A LIFE THAT MATTERS

DAVE DONALDSON

& TERRY GLASPEY

www.InfluencesResources.com

RELENTLESS

Published in association with The Quadrivium Group—Orlando, FL
info@TheQuadriviumGroup.com

Developmental Editing: Ben Stroup, BenStroup.com—Greenbrier, TN
Copyediting, proofreading, interior design: KLOPublishing.com
and www.theDESKonline.com
Cover Design: RootRadius, LLC—Ackworth, GA

ISBN: 978-1-93669-992-6

13 14 15 16 • 5 4 3 2 1

Printed in United States of America

To Dr. Thomas Trask, Glen Cole, Tommy Barnett,
Dr. Robert Spence, and John Maxwell
for inspiring the Donaldson brothers,
our Convoy of Hope team,
and faithful partners to a
relentless passion to feed the world.

Contents

Acknowledgments

T his book was made possible because of Dr. George O. Wood and Sol Arledge's vision to launch the new publishing effort, Influence Resources, led by a wonderful team, Steve and Susan Blount, Justin Lathrop, and editor, Ben Stroup. Special thanks goes to Justin for first envisioning this book and encouraging me to pursue the theme: relentless.

In addition, I am grateful to Harvest House Publishers and co-author, Terry Glaspey, for their investment in *The Compassion Revolution* book, which inspired and became a valued resource for *Relentless*.

Many of the inspirational stories throughout *Relentless* are from my work with Convoy of Hope, which has provided hope and help to over 50 million people. This was made possible through a constellation of partnerships including churches, organizations, businesses, government agencies, faithful donors, and a vast army of *Relentless* volunteers.

My heart is also filled with gratitude toward God for blessing me with such a wonderful family. This includes my dad and grandmother, who live in heaven, my mom, Betty, and her husband, Bernie, and my siblings, Hal, Steve, and Susan. And my better two-thirds, Kristy, who plants my feet but gives me wings to fly. Together we are raising four *Relentless* children, Breahn, Barbara, David, and Brooke.

CONGRESSIONAL ADDRESS

COMMENDATION OF CONVOY OF HOPE

Mr. Speaker, one of the great economic fallacies of our time is that if government doesn't do something, no one will. This disastrous fallacy underlies much of our national debate concerning heath care, education, poverty, housing, and disaster relief, to name just a few issues.

But today I rise to applaud an organization that stands in stark refutation of that fallacy. Convoy of Hope, a private charity in Springfield, Missouri, does so much to help so many communities that the term "charity" doesn't begin to describe it. In fact, Convoy of Hope is equal parts grocer, clothier, heath-care provider, first responder, educator, and logistics expert. It works with communities in America and around the world bringing together local charities, businesses, churches, and government agencies to alleviate poverty and help people in the wake of disasters.

In other words, it is a real community organizer! The tremendous scope of its activities serves as a reminder that government is neither the sole nor the best provider of goods and services to people in need.

Mr. Speaker, I recently had the privilege of touring Convoy of Hope's headquarters and distribution center. It was a humbling but deeply encouraging experience, as I learned the full extent of its charitable outreach. Frankly, I've never seen an organization so focused, efficient, and poised to do tremendous good for so many people.

First, some background: Convoy of Hope was founded by Hal and David Donaldson in 1994, who as young boys suffered the death of their father and subsequent poverty. But both men were struck by the outpouring of support their family received during that time; local churches and the community provided food and shelter. As a result, the two brothers both developed a deep sense of responsibility to help others in need.

In the years since, Convoy of Hope has helped more than 50 million individuals in more than one hundred countries—giving away nearly $300 million worth of food and supplies in the process.

Today, Convoy of Hope describes its mission as a global movement focused on four keys:

- *Children's feeding initiatives*: The organization's overriding goal is to alleviate child hunger worldwide, providing food and clean water while also teaching agricultural techniques.
- *Community outreach*: Convoy of Hope coordinates dozens of community events annually with thousands of volunteers and guests. These events involve free groceries; job and health fairs; and activities for children. As always, this outreach is available to all, without regard to age, race, physical appearance, or religion.
- *Disaster response*: From an earthquake in Haiti to a

tsunami in Indonesia to tornadoes in the American south, Convoy of Hope is a proven first responder. With its fleet of tractor trailers, 300,000 square foot warehouse, and high-tech mobile command center, it efficiently leverages relationships with private industry to help victims of worldwide disasters.

- *Partner resourcing*: Convoy of Hope supports hundreds of like-minded organizations throughout the world, providing them with the food and supplies needed to help their communities. In this way Convoy of Hope consistently promotes local control, results, and accountability—while demonstrating humility and a willingness to let others shine and take credit in local communities.

Unlike government bureaucracies and many top-heavy private charities, Convoy of Hope applies a uniquely results-oriented approach to serving people. You won't find bloated salaries or patronage jobs at Convoy of Hope, nor will you find tony offices in New York or Los Angeles like so many nonprofits. In fact, the organization regularly spends only about 10 percent of its budget on overhead (a very low ratio in the nonprofit world), while employing a small staff of approximately eighty-five employees. Watchdog group Charity Navigator consistently gives Convoy of Hope high marks for both its financial acumen and transparency.

Convoy of Hope also stretches its resources by developing strategic partnerships with private sector corporations, many of which provide in-kind donations of goods or services. This allows Convoy of Hope to offer a win-win proposition to prospective corporate donors: companies benefit from donating needed goods or services already in their inventory or area of expertise, while Convoy of Hope benefits from receiving the supplies and services it needs without paying retail prices. Its corporate donors—including Coca-Cola; Nestle; Proctor & Gamble; Georgia Pacific; Cargill; Del Monte; and FedEx—donate everything from building supplies to bottled water to toiletries. These partnerships with successful private companies demonstrate an entrepreneurial mindset that enables Convoy of Hope to help more people with less overhead.

Its massive distribution center and headquarters are located strategically in Missouri, where its fleet of trucks can dispatch quickly anywhere in America. It also operates six international distribution centers for logistical efficiency. By contrast, many government agencies purposely locate offices and facilities in different states at the clear expense of efficiency, solely to curry funding support from as many members of Congress and Senators as possible.

The next step for Convoy of Hope is an audacious one: a fifty state tour beginning in May designed to address poverty across the United States. The "Convoy of Hope Tour" will provide an average of $1 million in goods and services to a community in a single day. Convoy of Hope's fleet of eighteen-wheel trucks will roll through every state, providing a wide variety of goods and practical services to those in need, including:

- Groceries
- Job counseling
- Clothing
- Dental care
- Breast cancer screenings
- Haircuts
- Family portraits
- Children's activities
- Prayer and connections with local churches

Finally, while Convoy of Hope is a Christian-based organization, it is nondenominational and strongly non-political in its approach, helping those in need without imposing their faith. Convoy of Hope employees simply believe their faith compels them to help their fellow man. This commonsense dictum guides and infuses everything that Convoy of Hope does.

Mr. Speaker, in conclusion let me state unequivocally that Convoy of Hope is doing tremendous work on behalf of mankind. I wish everyone at Convoy of Hope (and their donors) best wishes for great success with their upcoming Tour. It's hard to imagine a government agency operating as efficiently, as nimbly, or even as cheerfully as Convoy of Hope. I truly believe it should serve as a model for private, nongovernmental solutions to poverty and its attendant ills.

—Dr. Ron Paul
Congressman and Former Presidential Candidate

RELENTLESS

WANTED: RESTLESS FOR THE POOR

T he dangling sign from the door of the employment office read: *Wanted! Restless for the Poor. Apply Inside.*

Curious but more cautious, he briskly walked past the door again where this odd sign had hung for several days. He wondered, Why hasn't that job been filled yet? There must be plenty of people who are restless for the poor like me but are far more qualified. Isn't this the job of government anyway to be the social safety net? What about the trained clergy who are paid to do this kind of thing? Somebody out there must be missing his or her calling!

Mysteriously, each question he posed only slowed his pace and desired retreat from the lure of the office. It felt like he was caught in the tractor beam from Star Trek, pulling him ever closer. Finally, he relented and walked towards the dangling sign and nervously stopped at the door.

Sighing deeply, he turned the knob only to enter a vacant room. "Is anyone here?" he asked, hoping for no reply. Fortunately, his question was greeted only by sounds of creaking walls and the sign now flapping in the wind. Peering around the dimly lit room, he could only see a small table and gold lettered writings on the wall. Moving closer he read the inscriptions aloud:

> The Spirit of the Lord God is upon me, because the Lord has anointed me; he has sent me to bring good news to the oppressed, to bind up the broken hearted, to proclaim liberty to the captives, and release to the prisoners; to proclaim the year of the Lord's favor.

It's you I have been waiting for!

Your Job Description: Preach the Good News to the Poor

Experience Required: None

Starting Date: Now

Management: Jesus

For a moment he stood motionless, paralyzed by the thought that all along Jesus had been waiting for him to carry his mantle of compassion to the oppressed, brokenhearted, and captives of poverty. He admitted, "Jesus was trying to get my attention through restlessness and an unfulfilled passion to make my life count. Yet, I could not hear Him because I was listening to so many other voices vying for my attention."

For too long he had hidden behind the cynicism toward Christians by claiming Jesus called us to care for the least of these but followers of Jesus seem to care the least about anyone but themselves. He thought to himself, "I've huddled with the skeptics who question why so much money is raised for the poor by charities but the gap only widens between the rich and the poor. And what about government sinking deeper into a sea of red ink while trying to mend society's brokenness?"

Even if he said yes to the invitation, the world's problems are big. How can one person possibly make a dent? Where would he begin? What would he do? It all seems like one big mosh pit of confusion and futility, so why even try?

But wait! The message on the wall said that Jesus was not waiting for other Christians, charities, or even government to take action. The invitation was available to anyone bold enough to preach the good news to the poor. Jesus hears the cries of the suffering. He is waiting for people to make a decision: Will they keep walking past the employment office and grow even more discontent, or shut up and get to work?

Even though the future seemed more uncertain than ever, he had a renewed sense that a fulfilling life awaited. Falling to his knees he whispered, "Jesus, I'm sorry you had to wait this long for me, but I'm now ready to surrender my life to you and your mission. Help me to learn from the poor, to defend them against injustice, to try and meet their physical needs, and most importantly, to share the eternal hope through your gift of salvation. Jesus, as I begin this new journey, please show me where to start, how I am to prepare, and where I should go. Amen."

Standing to his feet, he was drawn to the little table in the middle of the room and saw on top what appeared to be a large envelope. Immediately, he looked inside and pulled out a note that read:

Congratulations on accepting your new job! Inside is your employee manual, which will prepare you for the adventure ahead and the many unknowns and challenges you may face.

Anxious to get started, he turned the envelope upside down and shook it until a book dropped out and landed face down on the table. Flipping the book right side up, his eyes quickly read the employee manual's title: *Relentless: Join the Movement of Hope!*

Chapter 1

——

TEN REASONS
THE RELENTLESS GIVE US HOPE

Her lifeless eyes stared back at me through strands of matted hair. Layers of dirt from the Mathare Valley slums blushed her face and blotched her shredded white dress. She was perched on a rock with bare feet dangling above soil littered with glass and nails. I thought, *What a perfect photo for our newsletter and fundraising appeal.* As I became a human tripod to capture a photo of this poster child for poverty, a hand covered my camera lens. Looking up I discovered a Kenyan woman waving her finger at me and saying, "No!" Obviously, the little girl was her daughter and she did not approve of me taking her picture. What happened next would shake my world and forever change how I view the poor.

The little girl's mom walked over to her daughter and, taking a damp cloth, wiped the dirt off her face and then pushed her bangs away from her eyes. She straightened the girl's dress and brushed off the loose dirt to expose the beautiful white lace. Then turning toward me, the proud mom waved her hand to grant me permission to photograph her daughter. My immediate thought was, *You have ruined my picture and the opportunity to help children like yours.* But when I saw how proud the mom was of her photogenic daughter and how happy it made the daughter, I realized who was truly "the least of these." Had I dehumanized this little girl to the place where I preferred the photo over lifting her dignity? Wouldn't any mom, even one living in the slums of Africa, do what this mom had done?

Yes, there is a time and place to expose the squalor of poverty, hoping it will call people to a meaningful existence of sharing with those who lack the basic essentials of life. But we cross the line when we "cue the flies" to use someone's plight to build our status or that of our well-meaning cause or organization. If our goal is not to learn from the poor and affirm their value in God's eyes, then we are exploiting them, and our use of their faces and stories should be called "Poor-nography."

Most of what you are about to read I have learned from growing up poor and then learning from the poorest of the poor. One thing is certain: The poor believe the best of those who are trying to help them and their families live a life free of hunger, disease, violence, corruption, and hopelessness. They find much hope in people like Bob Goff and Katie Kilpatrick.

When Bob Goff learned that thousands of juveniles had been held in Ugandan jails for years without trials, he decided do something about it. He and his friend Charlie visited every juvenile jail in the country. They took the cases to court, won the cases, and emptied the jail cells. Thousands of kids were able to return to their homes and to normal lives.[1]

Over Christmas break her senior year in high school, senior class president and homecoming queen, Katie, took a short mission trip to Uganda. Her life was changed forever. When she saw the desperate needs of the people in Uganda, she left family and friends in Nashville, Tennessee, to help them. She established a sponsorship program to feed forty orphans, she adopted thirteen children to care for herself, and she developed a feeding program that provides food for 1,200 children each week. She gave up a comfortable life to care for the less fortunate of this world.[2]

On a warm Southern California day, a little girl decided to set up a stand and sell lemon popsicles in her front yard. After two weekends of sales, she made $27.00 and donated half of her proceeds to Convoy of Hope to help those in need. "It's better for other people to have food and clothes who don't have any, than to keep more for ourselves," Kate said. The $13.50 she sent to Convoy of Hope is enough money to feed a child for almost a month. It will help provide safe, clean water to drink and a better chance for a good education. By making popsicles out of lemons, eight-year-old Kate Kilpatrick was able to change the life of a child.[3]

Who are these people? They are the people we are looking for. We call them the Relentless. They give us much hope. Why? They truly believe they were born into this world with a purpose greater than serving themselves. In their DNA is a core value: to truly live you need to give. The world is desperate for them. They realize there has never been a time in history where it is so easy to help so many. We have wealth to spare, we have knowledge and resources like never before. We can travel the world in twenty-four hours and communicate around the world in seconds. The Relentless know this, and they are determined to take advantage of this moment in time to make a difference.

The Relentless embody ten rare and bold characteristics.

1. The Relentless believe they can sell sugar water and change the world.

A young college student sitting next to me on the plane peered over my shoulder as I watched a new video of Convoy of Hope's work in Haiti. He said to me, "I'm studying to be an engineer, not a social worker. But I want to make a difference in the world." I replied, "When Steve Jobs was trying to lure the CEO of PepsiCo, John Sculley, to run Apple, he said, 'John, do you want to spend the rest of your life selling sugar water, or do you want a chance to change the world?'" Looking at the young man I said, "Steve Jobs was wrong."

- You can sell sugar water and change the world!
- You can be an engineer and change the world!
- You can pump gas, wait on tables, or mow lawns and change the world!
- You can make a difference in the lives of others from wherever you live, work, and serve.

Quoting the words of the prophet Isaiah, Jesus declared, "The Spirit of the Lord is on me, because he has anointed me to preach good news to the poor. He has sent me to proclaim freedom for the prisoners and recovery of sight for the blind, to release the oppressed, to proclaim the year of the Lord's favor" (Luke 4:18–19). When the disciples posed the same question to Jesus, His response was to raise the bar even higher: "I tell you the truth, anyone who has faith in me will do what I have been doing. He will do even greater things than these, because I am going to the Father" (John 14:12).

The Relentless will stop at nothing short of changing the world.

2. The Relentless are committed to making the church more relevant and not abandoning it.

One nonprofit leader said to me, "Our organization is recruiting tons of young people who have given up on the church." This is a sad commentary. Perhaps these young people have given up because they have lost a vision of how amazing the church can be when it fulfills God's mission: to reach the brokenhearted, the oppressed, and the poor.

Bill Hybels wrote in his book, *Courageous Leadership*, "There is nothing like the local church when it's working right. Its beauty is indescribable. Its power is breathtaking. Its potential is unlimited. It comforts the grieving and heals the broken in the context of community. It builds bridges to seekers and offers truth to the confused. It provides resources for those in need and opens its arms to the forgotten, the downtrodden, the disillusioned. It breaks the chains of addictions, frees the oppressed, and offers belonging to the marginalized of this world. Whatever the capacity for human suffering, the church has a greater capacity for healing and wholeness. Still to this day, the potential of the local church is almost more than I can grasp. No other organization on earth is like the church. Nothing even comes close."[4]

God has blessed His church not only with abundant opportunities to help others but with abundant resources to do so. He has also called on His church to reach out to help the poor and suffering not just across the seas but across the street.

Do you think I'm exaggerating? As a woman and her young daughter left one of our Convoy of Hope outreaches I asked her, "Did you enjoy yourself today?" The young girl smiled as she raised a balloon in one hand and a candy cane in the other. "We've never been treated with such kindness," the mother said, her arm around her daughter. "Do you live in this area?" I asked. I wanted to be sure someone could follow up with further help. They pointed in the direction of a neighborhood close by.

"We live over there," the woman said. "In the neighborhood behind the church?" I asked. "No," the mother said a little more cautiously, "let me show you." They led me toward a dumpster and a broken-down bus behind the church.

As they approached the dumpster, the young girl pointed. "There," she said innocently, "we live there."

My heart collapsed when I looked behind the dumpster and saw a makeshift shelter of plywood and cardboard. Shocked and saddened, I reluctantly asked. "You live here?" They both nodded.

Jesus commanded us to care for the least of these, but I sometimes wonder how many of us would have to admit that we care more for ourselves than the least of these. The Relentless, however, are determined to be different. They are not going to give up on the church but will transform it into vibrant centers of hope and healing.

3. The Relentless offer the best help by bringing together people and solutions.

An African proverb says, "If you want to go fast, go alone. If you want to go far, go together." Kingdom-minded diplomats realize that by building bridges across denominational, cultural, and ethnic lines, their own ministries are enriched and enlarged. They know that only by joining hands and resources and time and energy will we be able to touch the corners of this earth with God's love.

People came together and found a solution for one of America's crowning achievements: The Transcontinental Railroad. Many experts predicted it could never be done, but the Union Pacific and the Central Pacific brought together competing leaders and companies to build the 3,500 miles of track to link the West and East Coasts.[5] What would have taken a family six months in a hazardous stagecoach or wagon train now only took six days.

The Relentless are busy building something similar to the Transcontinental Railroad in their own communities. They are unifying churches, businesses, nonprofit organizations, and government agencies around a movement of hope. They are bringing people and ideas together around a common goal of helping the helpless. And they are doing it with passion and purpose. Nothing is going to stop them.

I am tremendously encouraged when Rick Warren writes that a growing movement of churches are becoming centers that connect people to meet needs. He suggests that "the first reformation . . . was about creeds; this one's going to be about our deeds. The first one divided the church; this time it will unify the church."[6]

4. The Relentless humbly serve local leaders, so they are encouraged and better equipped.

Unfortunately, many people in third-world countries often believe that people from first-world countries who come to help them are well-meaning but are bent on managing projects rather than serving where they are needed most.

Walking through immigration in Ethiopia, I learned I had mistakenly omitted the answers to a few questions on the admittance form. The security agent asked, "Occupation?" I replied with a little chuckle, "No, I am just visiting." This is the mindset of the Relentless. They travel to the ends of the earth to give of themselves, not as occupiers but as visitors.

When the Relentless have an opportunity to serve in another culture, they humbly evaluate, "How can I boost the confidence of these people? How can I improve their ability to fish for themselves?" This is something we are always careful to consider at Convoy of Hope. For example, if we imported rice into Haiti at below-market price it would practically stop the farming and drain jobs, income, and the dignity of Haitians by diminishing opportunities for them to become wage earners for their families.

{ *In the time it takes you to read this sentence, four children will lose a parent due to poverty, disease, violence, or a natural disaster.* }

Instead, we and other organizations are working in Haiti to provide seed and to teach farmers techniques to better nourish the soil and expand their harvest. In return, the farmers agree to give part of the income from the crops to their churches and part to the feed hungry children. This is what I call win-win!

The Relentless slip into the sandals of Jesus and follow His example:

> Do nothing out of selfish ambition or vain conceit, but in humility consider others better than yourselves. Each of you should look not only to your own interests, but also to the interests of the others. Your attitude should be the same as that of Christ Jesus: Who, being in very nature God, did not consider equality with God something to be grasped, but made himself nothing, taking the very nature of a servant. (Phil. 2:3–7a)

5. The Relentless hold charities accountable for the funds they raise to help others.

For some charities and professional fundraisers, the poor have become their poster child in a lucrative industry that raises huge amounts of money using their images of suffering. The unfortunate reality is that sometimes only a small fraction of this money is actually used to help the suffering people in the pictures. I call these self-absorbed fundraisers "panhandlers in a suit." They are no different than a panhandler on the street who asks for bus fare and then spends the money people give him on drugs, smokes, or a lottery ticket.

In the aftermath of the September 11 attacks, many charities set up funds for the families of victims of the terrorist attacks. They created public service announcements and sent out direct mail appeals for this purpose. People responded generously. Then, we learned from the *New York Times* that in some cases, a relatively small percentage of the donations actually made its way to the families. Donations were instead used to meet other general and administrative needs. Even though one could argue that these were legitimate and necessary long-term expenditures, many generous givers were left feeling as if they had been duped and cheated.[7]

The Relentless are not only generous in their giving, they make sure people and organizations do what they say they are going to do for the poor. "This is what the LORD says: Do what is just and right. Rescue from the hand of the oppressor the one who has been robbed" (Jer. 22:3).

6. The Relentless will do whatever it takes to defend others from injustice.

Those who are tempted to neglect the poor or take advantage of them should remember that God is the protector of those who cannot protect themselves: "I know that the LORD secures justice for the poor and upholds the cause of the needy" (Ps. 140:12). And He expects us to do the same: "Defend the cause of the weak and fatherless; maintain the rights of the poor and oppressed. Rescue the weak and needy; deliver them from the hand of the wicked" (Ps. 82:3–4).

In the time it takes you to read this sentence, four children will lose a parent due to poverty, disease, violence, or a natural disaster. There are 145 million orphans worldwide.[8] According to the United Nations, the number of children (between ages three and eighteen) living on the streets is impossible to know for sure but the numbers are in the tens of millions—and rising daily.[9] This alarming statistic should give us pause, especially when we consider the priority given to caring for orphans in Scripture.

13

"Religion that God our Father accepts as pure and faultless is this: to look after orphans and widows in their distress and to keep oneself from being polluted by the world" (James 1:27). This passage should be like a huge billboard in our path to remind us that caring for orphans is on God's short list of priorities.

The Relentless are prepared, like Job, to help snatch the world's orphans from the jaws of injustice:

> "Whoever heard me spoke well of me, and those who saw me commended me, because I rescued the poor who cried for help, and the fatherless who had none to assist him. . . . I was a father to the needy; I took up the case of the stranger. I broke the fangs of the wicked and snatched the victims from their teeth." (Job 29:11–12,16–17)

Millions of children worldwide are victims of child labor, human trafficking, and sexual exploitation. Each year nearly two million children are exploited in the global commercial sex trade.[10]

Millions more children, not yet victims, are not adequately protected against their predators due to the death of their parents or poverty. Many children are uniquely vulnerable to these threats, such as those living without family care, in the street, or in situations of conflict or natural disaster.[11]

The Relentless will do everything within their power to snatch these innocent children from the jaws of terror and a living hell. They align their burden with the heart of Jesus who invited the children to come to Him:

> Then they brought little children to Him, that He might touch them; but the disciples rebuked those who brought them. But when Jesus saw it, He was greatly displeased and

said to them, "Let the little children come to Me, and do not forbid them; for of such is the kingdom of God. Assuredly, I say to you, whoever does not receive the kingdom of God as a little child will by no means enter it." (Mark 10:13–15 NKJV)

7. The Relentless refuse to assume someone else will do it.

A television show performed a little experiment. An actor dressed as a businessman, walked down the street of a major American city, and suddenly collapsed right in the pathway of other walkers. The show's producers wanted to see how long he would lay there before someone helped. As the camera rolled, person after person walked by, mostly just giving a curious glance at the man who had collapsed on the sidewalk. Fifteen minutes passed, and then thirty. Finally, after forty-five minutes a fellow citizen stopped, stooped down . . . and stole his watch.

In his book, *The Tipping Point*, Malcolm Gladwell writes of experiments on "the bystander problem," trying to determine which situations would get bystanders to help out someone in need. In one experiment, a student alone in his dorm room staged an epileptic fit. The results were interesting. "When there was just one person next door, listening, that person rushed to the student's aid 85 percent of the time. But when subjects thought that there were four others also overhearing the seizure, they came to the student's aid only 31 percent of the time."[12] In other words, if people see others around them, they will assume that someone else is handling the problem and will decide not to get involved.

This hit close to home for me one day when I saw a pillar of smoke stretching toward the sky. It was only a few blocks away, so I ran over to see what was happening. Smoke was billowing out of the windows of a neighbor's burning home.

Looking around, I noticed several other neighbors watching the spectacle unfold. Approaching a couple standing across the street, I asked, "Has anyone called the fire department?" Folding their arms they replied, "Not sure. We assume so." "Well," I asked, "can I use your phone to make sure?" They agreed, and so I dialed 9-1-1.

After the emergency operator got the information about the fire and where it was located, I told her I assumed someone had already reported it but just wanted to make sure. "No," she said, "you are the first to call."

Then I started wondering if there might be anyone still in the home. Just then a woman emerged with a child in each hand. Now the "good neighbors" finally responded and got them out of harm's way. Moments later the fire engines arrived.

> The Relentless refuse to wear a Do Not Disturb! sign because they believe life is a series of divine appointments just waiting for them.

This experience taught me a valuable lesson: Never assume someone else is going to do the job! The Relentless refuse to wear a Do Not Disturb! sign because they believe life is a series of divine appointments just waiting for them. They take responsibility to meet needs.

8. The Relentless are willing and eager to learn from the poor.

The poor can teach us much, such as how to be grateful instead of selfish. The line was especially long at Costco one day as my wife and I joined the throng of shopping carts filled to overflowing with groceries stacked liked mountainous peaks. We could hear a growing chorus of fellow shoppers complaining because the pace of the checkers did not meet their expectations.

I couldn't help but contrast that moment from just a few days earlier when I had watched hungry children from Kenya's Mathare Valley slums joyfully waiting for a bowl of soup. I can assure you they did not complain if their soup did not arrive quickly enough.

The poor can also teach us about simple faith in God. One

African leader said to me, "We don't just believe in miracles, we depend on them every day." I have been among his people enough times to know it is true.

On a fact-finding trip through a small Central American nation, our bus was filled with pastors and business leaders from America. We were looking for ways to help the poor in this part of the world. After a long journey, we pulled up in front of an old orphanage where the children suddenly came rushing out of the dorms toward us. They were laughing, smiling, and jumping up and down. "Now that," said one of the pastors, "is a greeting!" The director of the orphanage approached us with nearly equal joy and excitement. "We have been praying for you!" he said. "Praying for us?" I asked. "Yes, we ran out of food yesterday, so the children have been praying for God to feed us."

Moments later, one of our Convoy of Hope vehicles arrived with rice, beans, and—oh yes—pizzas for everyone. Before our arrival, we knew nothing about the desperate needs of these children. But God knew, and He used us to answer the prayer of faith offered by these little ones.

People ask me, "Why do I feel closest to God when I am with the poor?" It is because the poor are so close to the heart of God. Mother Teresa put it this way, "The dying, the cripple, the mental, the unwanted, the unloved, they are Jesus in disguise."[13] The Relentless learn from the poor because they care about them and they spend time with them. Speaking of King Josiah, God declared, "He defended the cause of the poor and so all went well. Is that not what it means to know me?" (Jer. 22:16).

9. The Relentless avoid compassion fatigue because they are plugged into an unlimited power source.

The Relentless are plugged into God, the eternal source of wisdom, strength, joy, and compassion. Without Him to strengthen us, we cannot hope to keep ourselves focused and fueled to help others. We will quickly fall back on self-reliance, the desire for comfort, and the demand for short-term solutions.

Plugging into God's resources doesn't mean that we can solve all the world's problems. That is unrealistic. Nor does it mean that we will be able to completely avoid getting tired or weary in doing good. That is to be expected from time to time. But the Relentless avoid being overcome by compassion fatigue and losing heart because they remain plugged into the right source.

They cling to this promise from God: "If you spend yourselves in behalf of the hungry and satisfy the needs of the oppressed, then your light will rise in the darkness, and your night will become like the noonday. The LORD will guide you always; he will satisfy your needs in a sun-scorched land and will strengthen your frame. You will be like a well-watered garden, like a spring whose waters never fail" (Isa. 58:10–11).

10. The Relentless will go as far as they can see and then they will see farther.

Jesus said to His disciples, "Do you not say, 'Four months more and then the harvest'? I tell you, open your eyes and look at the fields! They are ripe for harvest" (John 4:35).

The world we live in is under siege—three billion are desperately poor, one billion hungry, millions are trafficked in human slavery, 10 million children die needlessly each year, wars and conflicts are wreaking havoc, pandemic diseases are spreading, ethnic hatred is flaming, and terrorism is growing. Most of our brothers and sisters in Christ in the developing world live in grinding poverty. And in the midst of this stands the Church of Jesus Christ in America, with resources, knowledge, and tools unequaled in the history of Christendom. I believe that we stand on the brink of a defining moment. We have a choice to make.[14]

Yes, the needs of this world are immense. Many days it feels like we are fighting a losing battle. Millions of adults and children alike are without adequate food, without clean water, without even the most rudimentary health care, without housing and shelter, and without much of a future. The needs are vast, and they are urgent. They surround the globe, reaching north and south and east and west. You may say, "But I'm only one person." That's right. You are only one person, but you are one person who can make a difference. Please don't wait to take that first step. The soil is already being prepared for you. Plant the seed, water it, and the fruits of your labor will become the seed for future opportunities to make a difference.

Steve Jobs describes the special DNA that thrives and drives the Relentless: "Here's to the crazy ones. The misfits. The rebels. The troublemakers. The round pegs in the square holes. The ones who see things differently. They're not fond of rules. . . . You can quote them, disagree with them, glorify or vilify them. About the only thing you can't do is ignore them. Because they change things. They push the human race forward. And while some may see them as the crazy ones, we see genius. Because the ones who are crazy enough to think that they can change the world, are the ones who do."[15]

You are the Relentless!

CHAPTER 1 IN REVIEW

Key Ideas

1. Those who are the Relentless give us hope.

2. Many people today are interested in making the church more relevant, not in abandoning it.

3. Today, people are far more interested and committed to stewardship than were their predecessors.

4. The Relentless are generally resilient and not likely to succumb to compassion fatigue.

5. People today are passionate and relentless about things that are important to God.

Discussion Questions

1. What are the people groups and/or issues about which you are most concerned?

2. Considering one of your responses above, what do you want to be your legacy of influence?

3. Identify some natural abilities and human resources you can use to help address some of the issues about which you are passionate.

4. Read John 14:12. What "greater things" does God want to do through you?

5. What does it mean to be part of the Relentless?

Chapter 2

IT'S A FOUR-LETTER WORD

You are with family and this is now your home."

These words, spoken by a member of my dad's church, marked the beginning of the long process of healing following Dad's death. That one little four-letter word *with* transformed the lives of what remained of our family and set us on a relentless course to help others discover the power of that word.

It all started on a hot, August evening in 1969. A local pastor huddled together with my brothers and me on a sidewalk outside the hotel where my family was living. I could tell something was seriously wrong just by the look in his eyes.

He glanced nervously back and forth between the three of us, as if trying to find the right words to say and to anticipate whether we would be able to accept them. He cleared his throat and then spoke the brief words that would change our lives forever.

"Your parents have been in an automobile accident that has killed your father." He searched our faces and found only shock and disbelief. "Your mother was in the car too, and she's in serious condition, but the doctors believe she will live."

At nine years old, I just didn't know how to process this news. People die in movies, but not in real life. And certainly not my dad. "You'll see," I assured myself, "in a few hours, they'll be home, and it will all be okay."

The tears flowed freely from my older brother's eyes and fell softly to the pavement as he tried unsuccessfully to be brave for his little brother. His tears rattled my confidence, but I refused to believe that I would not see my father again. "Where are Mom and Dad?" I pleaded to the pastor. "When are they coming back?" He gently took my shoulders in his hands, bent down to my level, and looked me squarely in the eyes. "David, your mom is going to be fine, but your dad is now in heaven."

I laid awake in the dark on many nights following that tragic day, wondering what would happen to us, where we would live, and who would watch over us. I worried that I would be separated from my brothers and sisters. After all, who would be willing to take in four children? We were moved from family to family for a number of days, and with each stop, I wondered if this would finally be the place where we would settle.

My grandmother assured us, "God is a Father to the fatherless, and He is watching over you." "How can God be our Father when He's all the way up in heaven?" I asked. "Just watch," she said, "He will fulfill His promise through His people." And He did.

That was the night I heard the words that opened this chapter, "You are *with* family and this is now your home."

I followed a stone path to a trailer owned by the Davis family. The Davises were faithful members of my dad's congregation. Bill Davis supervised the Sunday school, and his wife, Louvada, directed the women's ministry. The Davises didn't have a lot of money. They lived in a trailer with their two children, and we had often visited them there. But I knew this was unlike any previous visit. For now, weary from weeks of being fatherless, homeless, and moving about from house to house, we were going to settle down in a new place.

As I walked up the path to the trailer I clutched my suitcase in one hand and my pillow in the other while trying to chase away the fears that the Davises would come to their senses and send us away. But when I nervously reached up to knock on the door, it swung open. Mr. Davis was there, standing in the threshold with a warm, inviting smile. As we shuffled inside, Mr. Davis embraced each of us and spoke those life-changing words: "Welcome! You are with family, and this is now your home." That little word *with* meant that the Davis family was sharing more than their home with us; they were sharing their love with us. They were willing to share in our loss and in our pain.

Of course, this is what Jesus did for us. He left the glory of heaven and its five-star accommodations to come to earth to be with you and me and to challenge us to show compassion and love to others.

The Apostle Paul said:

Your attitude should be the same as that of Christ Jesus: Who, being in very nature God, did not consider equality with God as something to be grasped, but made himself nothing, taking the very nature of a servant, being made in human likeness. And being found in appearance as a man, he humbled himself and became obedient to death—even death on a cross! (Phil. 2:5–8)

In fact the word *compassion* means "to suffer with." Several times the Gospels reveal that Jesus was moved by compassion. "When He saw the multitudes, He was moved with compassion for them, because they were weary and scattered, like sheep having no shepherd" (Matt. 9:36 NKJV). The Greek word used in the original texts (*splangchna*) speaks of something happening deep inside us—in our intestines, our guts. It is a word of inner upheaval and violence. When Jesus saw needs, He did not simply feel a distant pity. No, He felt an internal churning of deepest sympathy and compassion. He became grief-stricken with the grieving; He hurt for the hurting. He did not turn away from the poor in disgust; He lived among them.

> For Jesus, being **with** the needy involved both a radical sacrifice for others and a lifestyle that swam against the culture's current to see lives transformed.

For Jesus, being *with* the needy involved both a radical sacrifice for others and a lifestyle that swam against the culture's current to see lives transformed. He taught us in His Word and by His life how to demonstrate compassion:

1. To have compassion for people we must be *with* people.

I know what you're thinking, "Wow, how profound!" It is profound and increasingly rare because many people today actually work at avoiding unexpected or impromptu encounters with others. Our busy schedules and preoccupied lifestyles drive us to practice being with people without the *with*.

My family and I have front row seats to this phenomenon every day. We live in a quaint cul-de-sac where we get an obligatory wave from our neighbors when they enter or exit their garages. It's like watching Batman escaping from the Bat Cave.

And now, through social networking, we can gain thousands of "withs without *withs*" through texting, Facebook, and Twitter. Is your house like mine, where receiving text messages from someone who is in the next room is normal? Magically, the handheld device asks about your day, announces that it's dinnertime, and of course reminds you of chores. Before you text me some smack, let me say social networking can be one of the best tools for personal encounters because of the personal and instantaneous messaging. However, it can never substitute for being *with* a person, especially when that person is in need.

In 1979, Mother Teresa was presented with the Nobel Peace Prize. During the Who's Who banquet to honor her lifetime of achievement, she appeared wearing a simple Indian sari, more suited for a peasant than a prizewinner. In her gentle, somewhat feeble voice, she challenged the guests to "find the poor here, right in your own home, first, and then begin to love there, and find out about your next-door neighbor." She then paused and asked the audience, "Do you even know who they are?"

If Jesus had had access to social networking, He would have definitely used it to fulfill His mission on earth. But His knowing the human need for personal touch and warmth, it would have been in addition to and not instead of.

As theologian Karl Barth so vividly described it, "From the heights to the depth, from victory to defeat, from riches to poverty, from triumph to suffering, from life to death."[1] Jesus, who could probably have simply "fixed things" from on high, chose a different path. He became a servant to humanity. He became one of us and entered fully into our experience.

Think about it! Why did the creator of this vast universe decide to live on Earth? Jesus could have simply repaired man's sinful condition from heaven sitting in an easy chair and using a remote control. Or, since it was necessary for Him to die on the cross, rise from the dead, and ascend safely into heaven, why didn't He just take a short-term mission trip to Earth over a long Easter weekend? Why did He bother to spend thirty-three years on earth, and then die on the cross and rise from the dead?

Hebrews 4:15–16 says, "For we do not have a high priest who

is unable to empathize with our weaknesses, but we have one who has been tempted in every way, just as we are—yet was without sin. Let us then approach the throne of grace with confidence, so that we may receive mercy and find grace to help us in our time of need."

Talk about an example of *with* from high places! The Bible is saying God wanted to know what it is like to literally walk in our shoes. He was willing to do that so we could have a personal relationship with Him that is absent of fear, guilt, and awkwardness. As we experience a relationship *with* Him, we will want to relentlessly pursue relationships *with* others, especially those in need.

Jesus left the splendor and security of heaven to be *with* us. And sometimes the mission to be *with* the needy will call us to leave our security and safety and venture into uncertainty and discomfort as we follow God's call. I think about Abraham who left the security of his home in Ur to journey to the land of Canaan. Reflecting on what Abraham was called to do, Hebrews 11:8 tells us, "By faith Abraham, when called to go to a place he would later receive as his inheritance, obeyed and went, even though he did not know where he was going." When Abraham received the call, he did not receive elaborate instructions or directions. He did not know where he was going. The destination was not as important as knowing whom he was following.

Throughout Scripture, we see others who had to step out in faith and obedience, often giving up much of their comfort and security, in order to be with others in need. We see this pattern throughout history as well. Martin Luther left the monastery to take up the dangerous task of speaking against religious abuses and teaching the extent of God's grace and mercy. Dietrich Bonheoffer, who had fled Nazi Germany to the safety of the United States, was compelled to return and strengthen his countrymen, even though his decision eventually led to imprisonment and death. Rosa Parks vacated her safe place in the back of the bus to sit with white people in the front, thereby declaring equality and the need for justice.

For these relentless followers of God, being *with* others included a physical relocation. The *with* to which God is calling you and me may not always require a major geographical change, but it will require a radical commitment to be with the lonely and forgotten of society.

2. Being *with* people means showing respect for all people.

I was running late for a special church service in downtown Washington, D.C., dedicated to rallying Christians to help end poverty in America. As I ran up the front steps to the church, there were two young ladies waiting outside in the cold. I asked them, "Why aren't you going in?" One of them responded, "You see we are lesbians, and the usher told us we were not welcome."

Months later, I was at an outreach and a lady shared with me her excitement that a pastor had invited her to attend his church. She said, "I told the pastor I don't have clothes nice enough to attend. The pastor said, 'Jesus doesn't look at the outside, He looks at the inside. So you just come as you are.'"

The power of truly being *with* others is weakened every time we hide within the circle of our friends and refuse to venture out into a world of lonely and forgotten people who are left outside because they feel like a nobody in a somebody world. Of course, it is a blessing to have close friends and to spend time together doing the things that you all enjoy. Jesus had some close friends who were called the Sons of Thunder. But Jesus did not limit His relationships to those close friends. In fact, His primary purpose was to influence His traveling band to "go out into the highways and hedges, and compel them to come in" (Luke 14:23 NKJV).

Peter, the disciple of Jesus, said, "You do not show personal favoritism, but teach the way of God in truth" (Luke 20:21 NKJV).

Even the Pharisees, archenemies of Jesus, acknowledged, "You [Jesus] aren't swayed by men, because you pay no attention to who they are" (Matt. 22:16).

To Jesus, truly being *with* people was not an act of bending toward the underprivileged from a privileged position; it was not an act of reaching out from on high to those who were less fortunate below; it was not a gesture of sympathy or pity for those who had failed to make it on their own. The hand that feeds and the hand that receives are both hands held by God, knitted together for His purposes, co-laborers in His work of demonstrating the glory and justice of God's kingdom. As the apostle Paul reminds us, "There is neither Jew nor Greek, slave nor free, male nor female, for you are all one in Christ Jesus" (Gal. 3:28).

Jesus had the widest peripheral vision possible when it came to being with people. "When he saw the crowds, he had compassion on them, because they were harassed and helpless, like sheep without a shepherd" (Matt. 9:36). I'm sure some in the crowd were victims of circumstance. By no choice of their own they had become orphaned, widowed, disabled, or recipients of neglect and abuse. Others bore the self-inflicted scars of destructive choices. He was relentless for both!

Can we show an attitude of "*with*" to a single mom who is milking the programs to garner more public funds? Are we moved when we see homeless people who have been hollowed out by drug addiction? Is there any compassion for the prisoner who has committed a heinous crime and now wastes away behind bars? Is there any compassion for the person who has wronged you or a member of your family?

In the ultimate demonstration of compassion, Jesus looked down from the cross and saw the very people who put Him there— the ones who betrayed Him, spat upon Him, and whipped His body into splinters of flesh. He gazed down upon a group of people, not a single one of them fully innocent, and prayed, "Father, forgive them, for they do not know what they are doing" (Luke 23:34).

Aren't you glad that Jesus is relentless about showing compassion to us regardless of what we have done or do?

3. The compassionate attitude of "with" is a lifestyle.

"Clothe yourselves with humility toward one another" (1 Pet. 5:5). When Peter said, "clothe yourselves," he was not referring to the kind of clothing you can put on or take off. Rather, he was encouraging his readers to make humility such an intrinsic part of their lives that it would be like skin—permanent, a part of them. When a willingness to truly be *with* people becomes a lifestyle, then each day becomes an adventure of divine appointments *with* others.

If a desire to be *with* the needy does not become a lifestyle, then we will search for the exit instead of the entrance almost every time. We all know people who are hurting or grieving, and we may feel awkward because we don't know what to say. We may doubt that we can really be of any help. We may even excuse ourselves by

> *When a willingness to truly be* with *people becomes a lifestyle, then each day becomes an adventure of divine appointments* with *others.*

thinking: they probably just want to be left alone. Truth be told, most of the time people don't need Dr. Phil to give them advice. They simply need someone they trust just to be with them during a difficult time.

When we see poverty and misfortune, we are tempted to turn away and pretend we don't notice. We may justify our inaction: "I already gave at the office," or "I help the poor through paying my taxes—isn't that what my tax dollars are for?" Or we may be moved to write a check and send it off to a good organization, which makes us feel as if we have done all we can do.

But God expects more than that from us. He wants us to enter into the spirit of *with*, to personally identify with the needs of our friends and of those we don't even know yet. To embrace the spirit of *with* as a lifestyle can be challenging because—like the Davis family—it conveys the mission to share in people's pain and sorrow. When you embrace that spirit you agree to carry some of their load.

The good news is that the willingness to truly identify *with* others by its very nature is contagious and will multiply the love of God like nothing else. The greatest way to bless the Lord for showing compassion to you is to share compassion *with* others. And one of the best ways for them to show gratitude to you is . . .you get the point.

The spirit of *with* came knocking at our door in the form of a sixteen-year-old girl named Barbara. She had been in foster care for many years and was desperately in need of a safe home. After we completed the required certification to become foster parents, a local agency asked us to consider inviting Barbara into our home.

To see if this would be the right fit for her, we made arrangements for her to come over for dinner. After the meal, we sat with Barbara on the couch and began asking her questions about herself in order to get acquainted. Immediately, she lifted her arms and crossed them in front of her face to seek protection. Obviously, she was frightened from years of neglect and verbal abuse. Our hearts melted as we saw this young girl like a beautiful flower closed up from all the pain she had suffered. By the end of the evening, it was apparent that God had knit our hearts together and this lovely teenage girl was supposed to join our family.

Days later, in anticipation of Barbara's arrival, we all peered out the windows watching as a car dropped her off. I will never forget seeing her approach our house, clearly nervous and hunched over as to hide from the fear that we would not want her or would decide not to keep her. My eyes filled with tears as I reflected back to the day when I walked up the stony path to the Davis' home. It had been nearly forty years earlier, but I was reliving it through this special moment.

With one hand Barbara towed along a suitcase filled with all her possessions, and with the other she clutched a pillow. Then as she reached for the door, I swung it open and stood on the threshold with the same warm and inviting smile that Bill Davis had given to me so many years ago.

As she stepped inside, we wrapped our arms around her and I said, "Welcome! You are now with family, and this is your home."

That once injured flower has blossomed into a beautiful woman who loves the Lord. Many times we have been asked (even by experts in the foster care system), "How did this transformation of Barbara happen?" "What's your secret?" I respond with a smile, "I hope you don't mind my saying it because it's a four-letter word." They anxiously ask, "What is it? Tell me, what is it?"

WITH.

CHAPTER 2 IN REVIEW

Key Ideas

1. For Jesus, "with" involved both a radical sacrifice for others and a lifestyle that swam against the culture's current to see lives transformed.

2. Today's concept of community often eliminates the personal interaction that was a part of community in Jesus' day.

3. God's call to all believers is a call to care for the lonely and forgotten in our world.

4. "With" is a lifestyle, not an event on the calendar. If "with" does not become a lifestyle, we will search for exits instead of entrances.

5. God's presence in our lives will transform our minds so that being with people is far more important than watching people.

Discussion Questions

1. What does the term *with* mean to you?

2. What are some situations in which your presence delivered hope and encouragement?

3. God's call is to care for the lonely and forgotten in our world. In what situations do you often encounter the lonely and forgotten? What is your plan to care for them?

4. What is the evidence of a lifestyle of "with"? Which of the characteristics you identified are missing from your life?

5. Read Romans 12:2. How is God transforming your mind? What attitudes and behaviors are undergoing a God-initiated transformation?

Chapter 3

STOP THE SUPERSIZING!

In his documentary *Super Size Me*, Morgan Spurlock decided to explore what would happen if he ate nothing but McDonald's food for thirty days. In only five days he gained almost ten pounds. By the time the thirty days were over, he had gained so much weight that it took fourteen months for him to return to his original weight. His experiment also had predictably bad effects on his mental and physical well-being. He had nearly supersized himself into serious liver dysfunction and severe depression.[1]

This film is an accurate commentary on the supersize epidemic sweeping modern culture, especially in the Western world. For example, according to the Self-Storage Association, Americans now possess more than two billion square feet of storage space outside our own homes. There are seven square feet of self-storage space for every man, woman, and child in the nation. Thus, it is physically possible that every American could stand—all at the same time—under the total canopy of self-storage roofing.[2]

Think about it. Even though we have expanded our home sizes by nearly one thousand square feet and families have grown smaller, we still need an additional two billion square feet of rented space to store our stuff. And this does not include the many families who can no longer shoehorn their cars into their garages because of all of the junk.

Over the past decade, there has been a 75 percent increase in rented storage space.[3] Nearly one in ten households in the United States—that is 10 percent—currently rent a self-storage unit, which has increased from one in seventeen since 1995. That's a 65 percent increase in the last fifteen years. The supersizing continues with little indication that our consumption habits are maintaining, let alone diminishing.

Believe me, I am not immune from the tendency to gather stuff. When my wife and I decided to do a spring-cleaning it became "storage wars" over what to keep and what to give away. It was so bad that I purchased a book to help me clean out the clutter, but now I can't find it because it got lost in all my clutter!

As I stated in the previous chapter, my point is not to bash people who possess nice things. I live in a nice home and drive a nice car. But can we dare to ask ourselves: Have I been brainwashed into thinking larger homes, luxury cars, and expensive gadgets are the path to a meaningful existence? Am I caught in a vicious cycle of believing that it's more blessed to receive than to give? Does comfort and convenience have such a tight grip on me that I can't even distinguish anymore between necessities and luxuries? Is it too radical for that person looking back at us in the mirror each morning to ask: How much is enough to live simply when most of the world doesn't have enough to survive?

> Can we dare to ask ourselves: Have I been brainwashed into thinking larger homes, luxury cars, and expensive gadgets are the path to a meaningful existence?

Sounding like one of the Old Testament prophets, James warns of the judgment to come on those who live in comfort while neglecting the needy: "Now listen, you rich people, weep and wail because of the misery that is coming upon you. Your wealth has rotted, and moths have eaten your clothes. Your gold and silver are corroded. Their corrosion will testify against you and eat your flesh like fire. You have hoarded wealth in the last days . . . You have lived on earth in luxury and self-indulgence. You have fattened yourselves in the day of slaughter" (James 5:1–3, 5).

In a world of supersizing, we need to develop what John Wesley called a theology of enough. He practiced this by determining how much he needed to live on—to meet his essentials—and then determined to give the rest away. This is a radically different way of thinking. Jesus warned His disciples about consumerism when He warned them about the lure of possessions possessing them. Instead of hoarding their wealth, Jesus challenged them to give to those who needed it most: "Sell your possessions and give to the poor. Provide purses for yourselves that will not wear out, a treasure in heaven that will not be exhausted, where no thief comes near and no moth destroys. For where your treasure is, there your heart will be also" (Luke 12:33–34).

PLEASE KEEP THE TAGS!

I remember kneeling down to help a needy girl living in Kenya's Mathare Valley slums put on a brand-new pair of shoes. Her face beamed as I slipped on first one and then the other shoe. But when I reached down to tear off the price tags that were still attached, she began to cry. Confused, I asked her teacher why she was upset. "Well," said the teacher "she has never had anything new before, and the tags are the proof. So please keep the tags!" I immediately apologized and tied those tags right back on. The girl's face lit up again.

I fought back tears as I thought about our walk-in closets and the variety of shoes and clothes that reflect our every whim of fashion. We spend thousands of dollars to keep current with the latest styles while many in the world have but one change of clothes and walk through rocks and glass without one pair of shoes.

When I returned a couple months later the girl's shiny black shoes were now flocked with dust from the slums yet to my delight and amazement, the tags were still hanging from the shoes!

It was such a small gift, but it was life changing for this little girl. Can you imagine the impact we might achieve if more Christians adopted a theology of enough, a value system based on giving away what we do not need? What would happen if we screamed at ourselves in the mirror, "Stop the Supersizing!" and passed on that purchase of a new car, clothing, electronic gadget, or daily lattes to make room in our budget for the poor?

I will admit that it is easier said than done because the cultural current of supersizing is not only a personal epidemic but a pandemic infecting every sector of society.

CORPORATE GREED

The last thirty years have brought about several prominent examples of corporations that might be more accurately described as Ponzi schemes selling phony income and balance sheets. Shareholders lost nearly $11 billion when Enron's stock price, which hit a high of United States $90 per share in mid-2000, plummeted to less than $1 by the end of November 2001.[4]

Enron's nontransparent financial statements did not clearly depict its operations and finances with shareholders and analysts. Even after auditors uncovered their schemes, Kenneth Lay, who founded Enron in 1985, encouraged his accountants to "keep making us millions."[5]

TOO BIG TO FAIL

And this was a prelude to a too-big-to-fail doctrine that made the financial system even riskier when the government promised to bail out the biggest banking institutions, especially if they helped people realize the American Dream, which is most commonly associated with owning a home.

I was sitting at a table in Panera Bread when a nicely dressed man approached me with a photo album. He told me, "When I brought my family to this nation, I was told that success was to own your own home. So, my wife and I found a home for sale that we loved and the mortgage broker helped us buy it. But now I have missed several payments, and we must turn it back over to the bank this week."

As he painfully flipped through the photos of this spacious million dollar home, tears dripped down his cheeks onto the pages. I felt sorry for the man but was also curious as to how he was able to buy this opulent home. He told me that he made approximately $80,000 a year after taxes, but the bank agent qualified him anyway because it was an interest-only loan that would begin with low interest and then graduate over time with the hopes that his company would become more prosperous. Tragically, this man's story has become the plight of millions of families who have been evicted from their dream homes.

The injustice runs even deeper for people tricked into signing loans through questionable practices that helped people qualify for loans that were truly too good to be true. Worse, everyone involved in the process was encouraged to take a risk on behalf of the robust

American economy, even if it was unfounded. All told, roughly four million families lost their homes to foreclosure between the beginning of 2007 and early 2012.[6]

Foreclosures accelerated the fall of property values, helping to spur more foreclosures. These losses brought the financial system to the brink of collapse in the fall of 2008. The steep recession that followed led to a landslide of mortgage delinquencies, as homeowners who lost their jobs often lost their homes. Tens of millions of others found themselves in homes worth less than their mortgages, unable to sell or refinance.

GOVERNMENT—TOO BIG TO SUCCEED

The president of Sojourners, Jim Wallis, says that the federal budget is a moral document. But it becomes immoral when policymakers believe they are wiser at spending our money than we are. Yes, history does repeat itself and taxation without representation now stretches from sea to shining sea. What happens when politicians (who determine our spending priorities) are elected by making promises to voters and lobbyists that will require public funds for them to get re-elected?

Of course, there are many upright policy makers who won't be bought, but isn't this like asking the fox to guard the hen house? Here's the point! Without holding these leaders accountable to God-honoring priorities—including a balanced budget—the system alone will always lead to the runaway train of tax-and-spend along with supersized debt. Forgive the poor grammar but: HERE WE IS!

Let's use an astronomical analogy about today's debt: If you stack up fifteen trillion one-dollar bills, the pile would stretch to the moon and back twice. If one trillion one-dollar bills reach up to 70,000 miles, then fifteen trillion bills reach over 1 million miles. The moon is 250,000 miles away, making a round-trip to the moon 500,000 miles. Thus, the stack is about two earth to moon round-trips.[7]

Thirty years ago, the US national debt was approximately fourteen times smaller than it is today. It took from the presidency of George Washington to the presidency of Ronald Reagan for the US government to accumulate one trillion dollars of debt. Since then, we have added more than $13 trillion of additional debt. The United States government is responsible for more than one third of all the government debt in the entire world. If you divide up the national debt equally among all US households, each one owes over $125,000.

Sadly, $15 trillion is such an outrageous number that it doesn't mean anything to anybody. So let's personalize the debt. When you divide the amount the US owes creditors by the population, the national debt equals over $50,000 per person. For real time data on the United States debt and how that breaks down for each household and person go to http://www.debtclocks.com/.

This is a wakeup call to the Relentless to join the fight over the federal budget and the out-of-control, supersized national debt. If you think it doesn't affect you, then think again! Approximately 10 percent of our total tax revenues go toward paying the interest on the debt alone.[8] The interest costs are now more than what the federal government spends on education, housing, transportation, environment, veteran's programs, homeland security, and agriculture combined.

How does paying ten cents of every dollar for interest on debt affect you and what your children may inherit?

The 10 percent used to pay the interest on the federal tax bill is lost. These are substantial funds that could be re-invested in education, job creation, and training for individuals who are currently unemployable because their skills are outdated.

It puts a heavy drag on the economy because 10 percent of potential consumer spending on goods and services is lost.

The interest on the debt is added to the deficit each year. About 5 percent of the budget is allocated to debt interest payments. By 2020, the interest payment is projected to quadruple to $840 billion, making it the fourth largest budget item.

The above items will decrease tax revenue, thereby further increasing the deficit. As the debt continues to grow, creditors can become concerned about how the US government plans to repay it. In 2011, this threat was ramped up when the S&P lowered America's long-term sovereign credit rating to AA+ from AAA. Over time, these creditors will expect higher interest payments to provide a greater return for their increased perceived risk. Higher interest costs will slow economic growth.

While meeting with Congressman Paul and his wife, we discussed the national debt and its effect on each of us. Doctor Paul said, "As long as we live above our means, we are destined to live below our means." But former President, Bill Clinton, reminded us in his inaugural address that "There is nothing wrong in America that can't be fixed with what is right in America."

The result of all this is that the poor will be poorer. United States sponsored programs that are proven to reduce poverty in America and around the globe will need to be eliminated or drastically cut.

Some Christians contend that the local church should bear the responsibility of the poor rather than the government. They say that the faith community is waiting in the wings and will fill the need if the government would step aside. But, realistically, most churches lack the capacity to care for their own flock let alone the masses on the welfare rolls. In a perfect world, it would require the federal government to maintain its safety-net programs while churches and faith-based charities strengthened and expanded their efforts to care for the "least of these."

INFLUENCING GOVERNMENT AS PARTNERS

Of course, many faith-based groups are leery about partnering with the government because of possible intrusion and loss of control. Many experts will tell you that unless there is a firewall in place, receiving public funds can become a slippery slope towards compromising the church's message and methodology. Ronald Reagan warned, "If you get in the same bed with government, you may not get a good night's sleep."

I have served on a government commission and have helped and witnessed many churches and other faith-based organizations effectively collaborate with federal and local agencies to help the needy without any pressure to change their mission and methods. Let's be clear: for millions of hurting people the government—not the church—is their center of hope because it provides what they need to live a sustainable life. Therefore, for faith communities not to compete for public funds and become the recommended service means the poor must continue to use the secular agencies approved, outsourced, and managed by the government.

And to their credit, several presidents have led the charge to level the playing field so that faith-based groups can compete for public funds and become the recommended social service provider if they can make the case for offering the best solutions. Government will not fund proselytizing, but it will support social services that are not directly evangelistic. Amy Sherman describes it as the difference between a brownie and a salad. A brownie represents groups that are entirely evangelistic and the ingredients cannot be separated; a salad may have a carrot representing soul-winning that the government will not fund, but the charity may also have lettuce, cucumbers, and olives that involve programs such as food distribution, water, housing, fiscal literacy, etc., that the government is willing to support with tax dollars.

{ *Supersized government needs to be changed and the Relentless can help accomplish that by running for office and serving in government positions at all levels.* }

Martin Luther King, Jr. said, "A social movement that just changes people is a revolt; one that changes both people and institutions is a revolution." Supersized government needs to be changed and the Relentless can help accomplish that by running for office and serving in government positions at all levels. In addition, the Relentless can participate in what I call the Revolution Strategy based on five R's:

- *Relationships*—Pray for and build genuine friendships with government leaders and their staffs.
- *Representation*—Build collaborations with like-minded, faith-based groups to become stronger advocates for the poor by influencing public policy and spending priorities.
- *Results*—Compete for public funds by submitting persuasive proposals and then deliver on the outcomes.
- *Resources*—Leverage private dollars raised with public resources.
- *Replication*—Establish models of success that consistently meet outcomes and make economic sense by helping people move from dependency to sustainability.

IT STARTS WITH ME!

From our glass houses it is easy to throw stones at leaders and institutions for supersizing our culture. The Relentless accept the challenge that the revolution starts with them and their daily choices. Let's join Habakkuk's prayer for America and the world: "I have heard all about you, Lord. I am filled with awe by your amazing works. In this time of our deep need, help us again as you did in years gone by. And in your anger, remember your mercy" (Hab. 3:2 NLT).

Our culture can be changed one person at a time when we embrace a lifestyle that lives out the truth that it is more blessed to give than to receive. At a Convoy of Hope outreach, our volunteers got a chance to practice this kind of generosity. In a small but very real way, they were able to show what it means to care enough to sacrifice some of their own comfort so that others might find a little comfort themselves.

It was a blisteringly cold fall day, the kind of day where the cold is insistent and inescapable. Our volunteers had come prepared. They left their homes dressed in warm jackets, stocking caps, gloves, and wool socks, ready to deal with the harsh conditions. But many of our guests from the community, who had lined up at the gate to wait for the event to open, were visibly shivering. Many of them didn't own any warm clothes.

One of the volunteers from a local church saw the disparity and decided to do something about it. Without any fanfare, he removed his coat and wrapped it around a shivering child. Others followed suit, taking off their hats, coats, and scarves and giving them to those who didn't have anything to protect themselves from the cold. It was the volunteers' turn to shiver for a while. But inside I know they were warmed by the joy of giving and that God's love and compassion was being supersized.

CHAPTER 3 IN REVIEW

Key Ideas

1. According to statistics, America has almost six square feet of storage space for every person in the country.

2. The theology of enough proposes that we live on as little as possible and give the remainder away.

3. The supersizing epidemic affects almost every aspect of society.

4. Churches are not immune to the supersizing epidemic. Church foreclosures were at a record high in 2011.

5. Because churches are strapped for cash, caring for the poor has become the responsibility of government programs.

Discussion Questions

1. What "stuff" are you collecting? For what purpose are you keeping it?

2. What would "living on as little as possible" look like for you? Is that a reasonable goal? Why or why not?

3. What areas of your life are most susceptible to supersizing?

4. Why is it becoming difficult for some ministries and non-profits to make ends meet? What changes do they need to make in order to survive?

5. Is caring for the poor the responsibility of the government or faith-based institutions? Explain your response.

Chapter 4

THE RICHEST PERSON IN THE CEMETERY

The skinny college dropout who founded Apple computers was born to unwed parents and then adopted by a blue-collar family. Steve Jobs later told an interviewer that his goal in life was "not to be the richest man in the cemetery but to leave the world a better place than he found it."[1] Fellow high-tech billionaire, Bill Gates, and his wife, Melinda, made that goal a reality by donating a fortune to "take on some tough problems: extreme poverty and poor health in developing countries."[2] Billionaires like Bill Gates, Warren Buffet, and the late Sam Walton, founder of Walmart, understood this timeless truth: If you want to live, then give!

Jesus showed His own generosity again and again throughout His ministry by offering His time and resources to help the needy. He clearly held onto possessions lightly, and He instructed His disciples to do the same: "Sell your possessions and give to the poor. Provide purses for yourselves that will not wear out, a treasure in heaven that will not be exhausted, where no thief comes near and no moth destroys. For where your treasure is, there your heart will be also" (Luke 12:33–34).

A life of sharing will not guarantee you'll be the richest person in the cemetery, which is only temporary. Rather, it guarantees you can live a fulfilled and meaningful life and one day die rich from depositing treasures in heaven.

Sharing is the only solution to bridging the widening gap between the rich and the poor. In his book, *Rich Christians in an Age of Hunger*, Ron Sider reminds us of our real situation: "The poorest 20% of the people (just over one billion) own 1% of the world's wealth . . . the richest 20% own 81%."[3] So, by sharing we can rescue our brothers and sisters from injustice, teach them to fish, and show them where to find the pond of opportunity. An African leader told me once that creating opportunity is making sure the ladder reaches all the way down to the poorest of the poor.

WE SHARE AN ISLAND

In the film *Castaway*, Tom Hanks plays Chuck, a FedEx employee whose cargo plane crashes near a deserted island in the South Pacific. Chuck soon realizes that he has been given up as lost and must find a way to fend for himself in his sometimes hostile environment. He is hungry and lonely but not willing to give up. He receives a wonderful boon when several of the FedEx packages he was carrying in the plane wash up on shore. These packages contain various items that he is able to use to survive, and he eventually concocts a way to escape from the island.

As I watched the film, the thought occurred to me: If I were marooned on a deserted island with other castaways and blessed with the resources to survive, would I share them with others so they could live, too? I think all of us, whether followers of Jesus or not would most certainly do so. What's my point?

We *do* live on an island; it's a global island called Earth. And we share this island with 7 billion other inhabitants. Nearly 4 billion of them live on less than two dollars a day. Nearly 1.5 million Americans live on two dollars a day or less. That includes some 2.8 million children.[4]

The apostle Paul spoke about this socio-economic gap and its remedy: "Our desire is not that others might be relieved while you are hard pressed, but that there might be equality. At the present time your plenty will supply what they need, so that in turn their plenty will supply what you need. Then there will be equality" (2 Cor. 8:13–14).

CLASS WARFARE OVER WELFARE

It must be underscored that Paul's call for equality is not a call for socialism where the government becomes Robin Hood by stealing (overtaxing the rich) to level the economic playing field so everyone has the same balance in their checking accounts. Neither is Paul stoking the fire for class warfare. He is not condemning the rich because he believes their wealth is the cause of poverty.

Paul is in no way saying because you drive a luxury car the poor drive a clunker or because you live in a nice home others are imprisoned in a fleabag shack. In truth, the Bible offers many examples of God blessing people with wealth from Abraham to King David, and it even relishes the splendor of Solomon's vast wealth. Jesus didn't condemn the rich because of their riches.

> From a biblical perspective, wealth is one of the many gifts from heaven's treasure chest that the Lord hopes to use to accomplish His master plan.

Instead, He confronted the rich young ruler because he loved his status and his wealth more than God's eternal priorities.

From a biblical perspective, wealth is one of the many gifts from heaven's treasure chest that the Lord hopes to use to accomplish His master plan. One potential major donor to our organization told me, "I could lose all of this money tomorrow, and it would not matter." And I replied, "God has blessed you with your wealth. It's not a question of losing it; it's a question of how you are going to use it."

Sider contends, "God wants every person and family to have equality of opportunity, at least to the point of having access to the resources necessary (land, money, education), so that by working responsibly they can earn a decent living and participate as dignified members of their community."[5] Doesn't that strike you as the way it should be? All God's children deserve a chance—an opportunity to have their basic needs met and to be able to improve their conditions by responsible labor.

Some banish the principle of equality of opportunity because they claim it's a liberal social agenda. They fail to realize that it's actually a biblical mandate first introduced to the people of Israel when they settled in the promise land: "When you harvest the harvest of your land, do not reap to the very edges of your field or gather the gleanings of your harvest. Leave them for the poor and the alien. I am the LORD Your God" (Lev. 23:22).

Yes, it's that simple! We all have a harvest field representing our time, talent, and resources. Your field might be small in comparison to others but the principle remains the same. We are to devote the first fruits or the first 10 percent of our income as our tithe to our local church. The people of Israel were instructed that no grain was to be harvested until the firstfruits offering was brought to the Lord (Lev. 23:14). In addition to that they were to allocate a corner of their fields for the poor. This was and is God's profit-sharing plan for meeting the needs of the local church and caring for the poor. I like to call it God's stimulus plan for sharers—He enlarges our harvest fields and our capacity to give even more.

HOW TO BECOME RICH BY SHARING

By now I hope you are asking, "How can I become rich by creating equality of opportunity for others?" The answer is found in a tiny but power-packed three-letter word—SOW! In the Bible, 2 Corinthians 9 is the SOW chapter. These verses hold the keys to unlocking untold riches: In sharing, you are *strategic, obedient,* and on your *way.*

Sharing Is Strategic

By sharing our abundance, the quality of life for the poor can be improved. Bill Gates said, "[Melinda and I] are both optimists. We believe by doing these things—focusing on a few big goals and working with our partners on innovative solutions—we can help every person get the chance to live a healthy, productive life."[6]

"Fifteen percent of the world in extreme poverty actually represents a big improvement. Fifty years ago, about 40 percent of the global population was poor. Then, in the 1960s and 1970s, in what is called the 'Green Revolution,' researchers created new seed varieties for rice, wheat, and maize (corn) that helped many farmers vastly improve their yields. In some places, like East Asia, food intake went up by as much as 50 percent. Globally, the price of wheat dropped by two-thirds. These changes saved countless lives and helped nations develop."[7]

By sharing your time, expertise, and resources, lives can be saved and improved. Later in this book, we will highlight how you can make a strategic difference in meeting the world's greatest needs.

Sharing is God's plan for church growth. Jesus said, "You are the light of the world. . . . Let your light shine before men, that they may see your good deeds and praise your Father in heaven" (Matt. 5:14–16).

Following Jesus' marching orders, Paul started a relief program to help the Jerusalem church alleviate poverty in their city. To fund the initiative, Paul traveled throughout Asia Minor asking Christians to donate funds to feed the hungry. In Romans 15:26 Paul states, "For

{ *Sharing is God's plan for church growth.* }

Macedonia and Achaia were pleased to make a contribution for the poor among the saints in Jerusalem," but the actual list of contributing churches is much longer. The list in Luke's Gospel includes delegates from Berea, Thessalonica, Derbe, and Asia.

As a result of Paul's journeys to help the suffering, churches were planted in Asia Minor and the gospel spread throughout the world.

The only way most people in the world will discover the good news of Jesus' love is when they see it demonstrated by the offer of a cup of water to the thirsty or a piece of bread for the hungry. Mother Teresa put it this way: "Let no one ever come to you without leaving better and happier. Be the living expression of God's kindness: kindness in your face, kindness in your eyes, kindness in your smile."

Paul declared there would be eternal results from sharing: "Because of the service by which you have proved yourselves, men will praise God" (2 Cor. 9:13). But *SOW*ing is a verb and requires actions of obedience: "Men will praise God for the obedience that accompanies your confession of the gospel of Christ" (2 Cor. 9:13).

Sharing Is Obedience

1. *It is the mark of a true follower of Christ.* The apostle John wondered if people who failed to be generous had experienced God's love in their hearts. "If anyone has material possessions and sees his brother in need but has no pity on him, how can the love of God be in him?" (1 John 3:17).

2. *It should be guilt free.* "Remember this: Whoever sows sparingly will also reap sparingly, and whoever sows generously

will also reap generously. Each man should give what he has decided in his heart to give, not reluctantly or under compulsion, for God loves a cheerful giver" (2 Cor. 9:6–8).

3. *It requires responsibility for the giver and receiver.* Sharing, if not offered wisely, can actually become counterproductive to the long-term good of the receiver. Irresponsible compassion can have a negative effect on how the poor estimate their personal value and their place in society.

At the same time, I believe there is a place for no-strings-attached sharing where you bless someone even if the help is unappreciated or wrongly used. Yes, there are times when I have given money to a person pleading for bus fare who squandered it on smokes, a six-pack, or a lottery ticket. At some outreaches, I have loaded groceries into cars nicer than mine. Yes, these things were hard to stomach, but each was an opportunity to help someone's world with the love of Jesus.

In some cases, the needy have lifelong disabilities that require a safety net to remain in place for a lengthy process and sometimes for the remainder of their lives. However, for most of the downtrodden, their setbacks are temporary and require us to view the safety net of our support as a trampoline to lift them and their families to live as sustainable and productive citizens.

Our mother lived this out before us. After the accident that killed my dad and debilitated my mom, our family slipped into poverty that was then undergirded by the welfare system. And for us, it was a safety net that I am grateful for to this day. As we will discuss in the next chapter the US government rightfully takes its share of the blame for supersizing a culture of dependency. But unlike many churches, at least it is there when tragedy strikes such as the death of a parent or spouse, the loss of job, illness, or disability. Perhaps the best way to think about the government welfare system is that for all its faults, it's like Noah's ark—it stinks, but it's still the best thing afloat.

For my mom, welfare was a temporary and vital assistance until she was healthy enough to learn the skills to secure a living wage job. Eventually, she entered a job-training program with Dow Chemical and became a senior buyer for the company.

As discussed earlier, in Bible times the owners of land were not to harvest the corners of their fields but to leave the grain for the poor. The grain was not handed to the poor; they had to take the initiative to meet their own needs. God could have commanded that a portion of the harvest be given to the poor, but instead He provided those in need with a way to work toward meeting their own needs and to experience the dignity that comes with labor.

Long-term irresponsible sharing—whether it is practiced by the government or the church—will breed a welfare mentality that erodes the self-worth of those who are supposedly being helped. Their incentive slackens, their dreams die, and survival becomes the only goal in life. As Robert Lupton reminds us, "When society subsidizes you for being noncontributory, it has added insult to your already injured self-esteem."[8] That said, this must not become an excuse for not reaching out and helping the poor. As one philosopher said, "Seldom resist an impulse to do something kind."

4. *It is one way to give thanks.* "This service that you perform is
    not only supplying the needs of God's people but is also over-
    flowing in many expressions of thanks to God." (2 Cor. 9:12)

God wants us to share with others out of a heart of thanksgiving. We give not out of guilt or manipulation but as an offering of praise to the Lord for providing us with food, clean water, clothing, shelter, and opportunity to improve our standard of living.

When we share out of a heart of thanksgiving, the Lord begins multi-tasking and blesses everyone involved. It's the way He has chosen to "open for you His good storehouse, the heavens, to give rain to your land in its season and to bless all the work of your hand; and you shall lend to many nations, but you shall not borrow" (Deut. 28:12 NASB).

{ *Let me sum it up this way: If God can get it through you, He will give it to you!* }

Let me sum it up this way: If God can get it through you, He will give it to you!

Sharing Is the Way to Breakthroughs and Blessings

If I tithe 10 percent to my local church, then I only have 90 percent left to pay my bills. And if I give another 10 percent to help the poor, then there is only 80 percent remaining. After paying taxes to Uncle Sam, I worry about slipping into poverty myself.

God's economy doesn't make sense in light of human understanding of economics. If you base your life on the world's view of money, you will miss God's blessing every time. Here is God's economics:

> Now he who supplies seed to the sower and bread for food will also supply and increase your store of seed and will enlarge the harvest of your righteousness. You will be made rich in every way so that you can be generous on every occasion, and through us your generosity will result in thanksgiving to God. (2 Cor. 9:10–11)

You may question my mathematical calculations when I say this, but just hear me out. If you faithfully tithe the first 10 percent of your income to your local church, and then leave a corner of your field for the poor, God will keep replenishing the seed (your resources). He will also enlarge your harvest field so the remaining 80 percent will exceed the 100 percent.

The best illustration of this is the story of Jesus feeding the five thousand. A large crowd gathered to hear Jesus teach. As the day wore on, Jesus became concerned that the crowd had gone too long without any food. He had been meeting their spiritual hunger, but He wanted to meet their physical hunger as well. He told His disciples to give the people something to eat.

I'm sure the disciples looked at each other in disbelief and said, "Say what? We don't have enough food to feed our own band of brothers, much less a mob of over five thousand?" Nor did the disciples have enough money to go and buy food. The need far exceeded the resources. In the same way, most people give with an attitude of apathy because they believe the need overwhelms their abilities and resources.

What the disciples were about to learn is that when you trust and obey God, His multitasking shifts into full speed. Think about it! Jesus was about to use a young lad's Happy Meal of five barley loaves of bread and two fish to overwhelm the need. The boy learned of the disciple's dilemma and decided to donate his lunch. From that point on, the biblical narration places the camera entirely on Jesus multiplying the bread and fish to feed the hungry masses.

But let's back up a moment and visualize the boy's amazement when he heard that his meager resources had fed a multitude of hungry people. Not only that, but when everyone had eaten there was more food left over than they had started with! Because the boy shared, his ordinary lunch became an extraordinary lunch! Like the young boy, we have a choice, too. We can play it safe, keep the firstfruits, and leave no corner of our field for the poor. If we choose to live like this, there is a good chance we will live an ordinary life. It might even be a good, ordinary life. Or we can choose to share and experience an extraordinary life that God has placed us on this planet to accomplish!

MAKING OUR "DASH" COUNT

Are we satisfied with living ordinary lives—holding tightly to everything we have, keeping it all, playing it safe? Or, do we yearn for extraordinary lives? Are we eager to experience the adventure of giving it all away to Jesus and watching Him multiply our lives to touch the multitudes with compassion?

When I lived in Washington, D.C., en route to my office I usually traveled past Arlington National Cemetery. There among the rolling hills are thousands of white marble headstones that commemorate the brave men and women who have given their lives to defend the freedoms we all enjoy. From time to time, I would stop at the cemetery to visit the graves of these soldiers and I noted when they were born and when they died.

The names and dates of each were different of course, but each one of those grave markers had one thing in common. All the epitaphs had a dash between the date the person was born and the date he or she died. That seemingly insignificant little dash represents the life of that person. Each was born on a certain date, and each died on a certain date, often in sacrificial service of the country they loved. Nevertheless, their lives were lived out in all the years between the dates.

You, too, have been blessed with a "dash" called life. You might be at the beginning, in the middle, or near the end of your dash. The question is: How will you use what is left? Once your final date is inscribed on the right side of the dash, will you have accomplished something for Jesus? What difference will your life have made?

Will you leave the world a better place than when you entered it? Will you have lived for yourself, or will you have given yourself for others? Mother Teresa reminds us, "At the end of life we will not be judged by how many diplomas we have received, how much money we have made, or how many great things we have done. We will be judged by, 'I was hungry and you gave me food to eat, I was naked and you clothed me, I was homeless and you took me in.'"[9]

THE RICHEST MAN I KNOW

When Convoy of Hope was approaching the threshold of serving fifty million people in America and around the globe, our team decided to host a celebration at the place where the vision all started in Concord, California. When that special day came, the banquet hall was filled with hundreds of guests ready for a family reunion that spanned more than forty years.

Within a stone's throw from that celebration hall were places that marked both joyful and painful memories for me. Not far away was our home, our schools, the church our dad pastored, and the site where he and mother had been struck by the drunk driver. Just down the road you could still stand where my siblings and I had peered into our mom's hospital room wondering if she would ever recover enough to take care of four young children.

> You, too, have been blessed with a "dash" called life. You might be at the beginning, in the middle, or near the end of your dash. The question is: How will you use what is left?

Now forty-three years later, my two brothers, sister, and I returned home to honor the Lord for turning our dad's death into life for over fifty million people. The evening program included well-wishes from dignitaries, a walk-down-memory-lane video, reports of Convoy's feeding program and disaster response, and special thanks to so many who had stood with us for many years. It was one of the highlights of my life.

But the most treasured moment was when a humble and tearful couple, nearing their eighties, made their way to the platform along with their family to receive the event's special honor. No, it wasn't a religious superstar, a top donor, a political figure, or a celebrity—it was the man who shared his little home and big heart with four emotionally bruised and frightened children. It was Bill Davis—the richest man I know.

CHAPTER 4 IN REVIEW

Key Ideas

1. Many wealthy people understand the adage, "If you want to live, then give."

2. Though Jesus had no earthly possessions, He was a giver.

3. The biblical model of caring for the poor is not a call to socialism through overtaxation.

4. Sharing is strategic, obedient, and on your way.

5. Being rich is more connected to caring than to owning.

Discussion Questions

1. What is your response to the adage, "If you want to live, then give"?

2. What were some of the "things" Jesus gave? How can you model your life after His example?

3. What would happen in our world if the biblical model of caring for the poor were implemented by churches and other faith-based organizations? Would more or less poor people be helped? Explain your response.

4. What is your plan for sharing your resources with others?

5. What is your definition of *rich*? What are some ways in which you already are rich?

Chapter 5

PRO-LIFE FOR THE POOR

No segment of the population has more closely identified itself with the pro-life message than Christians. We have stood up for the rights of the unborn with great fervor and passion. We have preached sermons, written books, and sometimes even taken to the streets to defend the rights of unborn children who cannot stand up for themselves. These are all valiant responses to God's mandate to rescue the weak and defend them (Ps. 82:4).

Without question the weakest and most defenseless are the children the Creator intended to be safely protected and nourished in their mothers' wombs. Even with sizable victories such as the ban on partial-birth abortion, congratulations would not be in order when in the land of life and liberty over one million children are snatched away each year before they can breathe their first breath.[1] If anything, we are not pro-life enough when it comes to rescuing and defending the most vulnerable.

WHOLE-LIFE

For the Relentless, the fight for the unborn may be the front lines, but it does not represent the entire battlefield. The full marching orders read: "Defend the cause of the weak and fatherless; maintain the rights of the poor and oppressed. Rescue the weak and needy; deliver them from the hand of the wicked" (Ps. 82:3–4). In short, our definition of what it means to be pro-life is too limited. We have tended to focus on one issue—abortion—and failed to think carefully enough about what it means to be consistently and thoroughly pro-life.

> We have tended to focus on one issue—abortion—and failed to think carefully enough about what it means to be consistently and thoroughly pro-life.

We must not only protect the child in the womb but also save the child living in the slums who is suffering from inadequate food, limited medical care, and subhuman living conditions. Jesus pleaded with his followers to become not only pro-life but whole-life in their service to the poor:

> "For I was hungry and you gave me something to eat, I was thirsty and you gave me something to drink, I was a stranger and you invited me in, I needed clothes and you clothed me, I was sick and you looked after me, I was in prison and you came to visit me.'" (Matt. 25:35–36)

THE FIGHT FOR TWO LIVES

Jesus says, "The thief comes only to steal and kill and destroy; I came that they may have life, and have it abundantly" (John 10:10 NASB). Jesus speaks of two lives in this passage: life eternal in heaven and life abundant on earth.

The first life, salvation from our sins and the promise of eternal life, only comes through accepting Jesus as our Lord and His free gift of forgiveness (John 14:6; Acts 4:12). Ultimately, for the poorest of the poor and the richest of the rich, this is not only the "good news" but the "best news."

For the second life, Jesus refers to the quality of life that He defines as abundant. My interpretation of abundance is having enough to meet the basic needs of our family (i.e., food, water, clothing, and shelter) and the opportunity for upward mobility (e.g., a good job). This standard of living can then generate the extra or abundance that should be used to lift others to sustainability and beyond. Prosperity is when you can lower the ladder to the lowest socioeconomic level.

Jesus warns that Satan's single aim is to block the path to both eternal life and abundant life through his arsenal of deceit and destruction. The enemy of man's eternal soul uses a full range of weapons to "blind the minds of the unbelieving so that they might not see . . . the glory of Christ" (2 Cor. 4:4 NASB).

For the poor, the Thief's strategy is to replace hope with despair through violence, disease, hunger, and other effects of poverty. The same evil was at work in the Nazi concentration camps, which killed six million Jews. The Thief was behind the slave trade that snatched millions of men, women, and children from their homes in Africa and transported them in slave ships across the Atlantic to either the Caribbean Islands or North or South America. Hundreds of thousands died en route.

And the booming sex trafficking industry of today proves that if the Enemy cannot kill human life, he will rob people of their potential and dignity by devaluing their place in society. Even in America, there is an emerging unspoken caste system that disrespects and discards the elderly by spewing the lie that they are no longer useful to society and, therefore, are expendable. This is all part of an orchestrated battle to defeat the Creator's pro-life plan penned by King David:

You made all the delicate, inner parts of my body and knit me together in my mother's womb. Thank you for making me so wonderfully complex! Your workmanship is marvelous—how well I know it. You watched me as I was being formed in utter seclusion; as I was woven together in the dark of the womb. You saw me before I was born. Every day of my life was recorded in your book. Every moment was laid out before a single day had passed. (Ps. 139:13–16 NLT)

Satan's other tactic is to divide whole life by stripping away the message of eternal life from the abundant life so as to be politically correct or culturally sensitive. Some would call this a social gospel. Remarkably, there is a strong movement of Christian churches and organizations swimming against this current to become advocates for the whole-life approach to missions.

For many faith-based charities, the pendulum has swung so far towards social activism that the spiritual transformation core of their mission can only be found in fine print or by dusting off an old newsletter. Peter, a disciple of Jesus, sounded the alarm, "Be self-controlled and alert. Your enemy the devil prowls around like a roaring lion looking for someone to devour" (1 Pet. 5:8). This warning is relevant to both vulnerable people and well-meaning institutions that can potentially place Jesus on the trading block for relief and development. There are many substantiated studies that prove the efficacy of the whole-life approach to outreach. Organizations such as Teen Challenge and Prison Fellowship can testify to what occurs when a cup of water is given in Jesus' name; it not only quenches a person's physical thirst but a holistic transformation occurs when that person's heart and habits are changed by a pro-life God.

WINNING THE BATTLE

In the coming chapters, you will read about the daunting battles we face in combating poverty, homelessness, hunger, human trafficking, euthanasia, and other great evils. You'll read about the heartrending realities faced by children and their families who live in extreme poverty, whether in the streets of Nairobi, Kenya, or the slums of Calcutta, India.

You'll also read the sad truth that many American families are also struggling with poverty and homelessness right in our own cities and towns. And you'll be brought face-to-face with the sad realities facing orphans here and abroad. As you read about some harsh truths, I hope that the bad news will not overshadow the good news that this battle for life is winnable.

This hope is based on at least three facts:

1. The battle is the Lord's.

God is the protector of those who cannot protect themselves, the provider for those who cannot provide for themselves, the one who fights for those who cannot fight for themselves. As the Psalmist reminds us, "The LORD secures justice for the poor and upholds the cause of the needy" (Ps. 140:12). If our trust, strength, wisdom, courage, and joy come from the Lord, then the outcome of the battle is fully in His hands.

2. Life fights for life.

One of the most inspiring attributes of mankind is the amazing will to survive under the worst imaginable conditions. This story below underscores how life fights for life.

A scientist placed a plant in a room with closed curtains and no light. He was experimenting to see how long it would take for the plant to die from lack of sunlight. As the days passed, the petals wilted and turned brown. What had once been a beautiful plant with stunning colors and a lovely scent was now struggling to survive.

Preparing to leave on a trip, the scientist checked his experiment one last time before he walked out the door. In his haste, he accidentally brushed against the curtain, and it was left slightly open, allowing a sliver of light to enter the dark room. He was in too much of a hurry to even notice.

When he returned, he expected to find the plant completely dead. But something mysterious had happened. The plant was not dead but very much alive. The scientist discovered that the branches of the plant were stretching out toward the thin beam of light that came through the slightly parted curtains. That little bit of light sustained the plant, even in nearly complete darkness.[2]

When it comes to serving the suffering, God combines our efforts to save and sustain lives with the DNA He placed in creation not only to survive but to thrive—to produce and prosper.

3. You are part of a God-sized plan.

As noted in chapter one, many experts said it could never be done but the Union Pacific from the West and the Central Pacific from the East ignored the doubters and laid rail across plains and high mountains until on May 10, 1869, the last spike was hammered at Promontory Summit, Utah. It was the culmination of a decade-long movement plagued with countless setbacks and sacrifice, but in the end it proudly knit together the United States of America by linking the Atlantic and Pacific coasts. This crowning achievement is called the Transcontinental Railroad.

As with the building of the Transcontinental Railroad there is a growing chorus of doubters who contend that nonprofit and government organizations are so independent that they will never collaborate and link assets to tackle the world's biggest problems. Some say that the issues are so diverse and complex that even the most relentless will never make a dent in alleviating suffering. As Tommy Barnett likes to say, "these people are 'doubt peddlers' always selling doubt that it can't be done."[3]

If we choose to buy the doubt peddlers' products then they will probably be right and conditions for the poor will only worsen. But for the Relentless, we see the world through a different lens, one where with God all things are possible. We believe there is a God-sized master plan and tracks are being laid by spirited comrades from the east, west, north, and south. At times we may feel like Captain America, a one-man army, but let's never forget that we are a band of brothers and sisters grafted into a pro-life mission who are fueled by a God who is relentless for the poor.

CHAPTER 5 IN REVIEW

Key Ideas

1. Pro-life is broader than the issue of abortion.

2. Life can be viewed as consisting of two realms: eternal life in heaven and abundant life on earth.

3. Satan's strategy is to rob people of the abundant life and, in doing so, make them doubt the reality of eternal life.

4. The key to abundant life is the pursuit of spiritual transformation.

5. The ongoing battle is winnable because the battle is the Lord's, those who are alive fight for life for others, and the Relentless are stepping up and becoming a part of the God-sized plan.

Discussion Questions

1. When you hear the phrase "pro-life" what comes to your mind? Is your understanding too narrow or too broad? Explain your response.

2. Which realm of life gets the most attention in your schedule—eternal life or abundant life? What are the risks of focusing on one to the exclusion of the other?

3. What can you do to help the downtrodden discover the joy of the abundant life?

4. What is your strategy for being spiritually transformed?

5. What is your personal role in the battle for the hurting in our world?

DADDY, I'M HUNGRY!

My daughter, Brooke, started to cry, "Daddy, I'm hungry." "I'm sorry," I tried to explain, "but we can't get any food right now." Our car was just one in a line of motionless vehicles, and the next exit was three or four miles away. Her cries grew louder. "Daddy, I'm hungry!" she wailed. I was helpless, as my hands grew tight on the steering wheel. "I'm sorry, baby, but Daddy can't do anything about it right now."

Then a realization awakened inside me. I was trying to explain to my daughter why she might have to go hungry for another hour. Yet I knew that if she could be patient, we would find food just down the road. But what if there wasn't any food at the next exit—or at the next exit or the next? What if I wasn't sure she would ever be able to eat again?

I suddenly saw in my mind moms and dads in Africa, India, or South America listening as their children cry for days on end because their stomachs are churning with hunger pains and the agony of starvation. I thought of parents watching helplessly as their children die a slow and agonizing death because they have no food to give them. This imaginative scenario is not an unusual occurrence in real life. All around the globe, mothers and fathers tuck their children into bed at night, wondering if they will be able to find food for them the next day.

More than 840 million people in the world are malnourished—799 million of them live in the developing world. Of these, more than 153 million are children under the age of five. And every year, 6 million of these infants and toddlers die as a result of hunger.[1] Others manage to find just enough food to keep them alive but not enough to sustain healthy bodies, so they develop crippling diseases and ailments and are destined to live out their days in pain and need.

Undernourishment negatively affects people's health, sense of hope, security, and overall ability to think and be productive. A lack of food can stunt growth, sap energy, and contribute to mental retardation. Good nutrition is the cornerstone for survival, health, and development. Well-nourished children perform better in school, grow into healthy adults, and in turn give their children a better start in life. Globally, more than one third of child deaths are attributable to undernutrition.[2]

It is almost impossible to get our minds around that magnitude of hunger so let me describe the need by showing you a word picture. If you add the number of children who died this week because they lack nutritious food, they would fill one of the largest stadiums in America—Michigan Stadium, which has a seating capacity for 107,501 fans—twice.[3] Think about it! Two stadiums filled with children dying every week because they lack what most in America can access at any moment.

The enormity of the problem can loom so large that we feel helpless and hopeless and choose to turn away. Looking into the face of a problem of this size takes guts and a selfless determination to do what John Wesley asked of his followers: "Put yourself in the place of the poor man and deal with him as you would have God deal with you."[4] If you dare do this it will bring home the reality of poverty and its effects. Rich Stearns, CEO of World Vision suggests we take a little mental experiment:

> Imagine what it would be like to awaken each morning wondering if you were going to eat. You have no money, there is no food available—you can't just run down to the grocery store. You would awake to the knowledge that every hour of your day must be obsessively devoted to the search for sustenance.[5]

The point here, as Cameron Strang likes to say, is to reject apathy and become relentless to the extent that you can't remain inactive about this devastating problem that consumes the lives of so many who desperately search for food to save themselves and their children.

And lest you think that hunger is only a problem overseas, take note of the fact that according to Bread for the World Institute, more than 1 in 5 children in America live in households that struggle to put food on the table. That's 16.2 million children. Some of these households frequently skip meals or eat too little because of inadequate money to buy food. Couple that with the US Census Bureau findings that 46.2 million people in America live below the poverty line, and you can see that the hunger problem needs to be addressed here at home as well as abroad.[6]

THERE IS A SOLUTION

When Jesus was on a preaching mission and being followed by multitudes who wanted to hear the good news of the gospel, He felt moved by their needs. He said to His disciples, "I have compassion for these people; they have already been with me three days and have nothing to eat. I do not want to send them away hungry, or they may collapse on the way" (Matt. 15:32). Surely Jesus feels the same way today: "I do not want to send them away hungry." So, He asked His disciples to solve the problem and today He is asking His followers to the same.

The good news is that world hunger is a solvable problem. Rich Stearns sums up the situation well: "The world can and does produce enough food to feed all of its 6.7 billion inhabitants. The problem is that both the food and the capacity to produce it are unequally distributed."[7] While others barely subsist (or fail in the struggle to subsist), Americans have an abundance of food. In the US, 30 to 50 percent of food—including fresh fruits and vegetables, milk, meat, and grain products—are wasted every year. The total value of that wasted food is more than $1 billion.[8] With all the pressing need for food, such a large amount of food being lost to waste and spoilage is a tragedy as well as a commentary on our extravagant lifestyles.

The United Nations Development Program estimates that the basic health and nutrition needs of the world's poorest poor could be met for an additional $13 billion dollars a year. Animal lovers in the US and Europe spend more than that on pet food each year.[9]

HOW CAN YOU SOLVE WORLD HUNGER?

The simple answer is to follow God's plan for ending world hunger, which is found in the ancient biblical practice of leaving a corner of one's field for the poor (Lev. 23:22). If we understand and follow this principle, it will challenge us to change some of our priorities so that more resources are available to feed the hungry and save the lives of innocent children and their families. If we each gave up a little of what we had, we would easily have the capacity to solve world hunger.

The Bible describes us all as having a field of fruits representing our time, talents, and resources (2 Cor. 9:6–8) that we use for our own sustenance but also to help the less fortunate. Yes, every person alive right now has a field of fruits! Granted there are those with bigger fields containing more fruit than others, but the principle of leaving a corner remains the same regardless of the size.

God says we are to give the firstfruits or the first 10 percent of our harvest or income to our local church (Mal. 3:10). But that should not be the sum total of our giving; it should be just the start. Generosity should be a way of life. Hebrew farmers were to make some of their produce available to the poor: "When you reap the harvest of your land, do not reap to the very edges of your field or gather the gleanings of your harvest. Leave them for the poor and the alien. I am the LORD your God" (Lev. 23:22). This practice is illustrated in the story of Ruth (Ruth 2). Her relative Boaz obeyed God's command and left the corners of his field unharvested and the upper branches of his fruit trees unpicked so that the poor would have an opportunity to find food and survive. Here are some ways you can "leave a corner of your field":

{ *Yes, every person alive right now has a field of fruits!* }

Give Money

Funds that are donated to Convoy of Hope global feeding program (www.convoyofhope.org) are multiplied many times due to the organization's low overhead.

Ken Jones, former pastor of Alamo Christian Assembly in the San Francisco Bay area asked, "What can my church do?" One day, Ken received a mailing from Convoy of Hope that spoke of the immense needs worldwide. His heart was moved to action, and he wanted to do something more than just receive an extra offering at the end of the church service. He wanted to do something that would have a lasting effect. For two months he preached every Sunday morning on God's compassion for the poor and our responsibility to help them.

All this preaching and teaching led up to a challenge—that members of the congregation would give up one day's wages in order to help the poor and the suffering. Virtually everyone in the church of two hundred members caught the vision, from teenagers with part-time jobs to senior citizens living on pensions. When the day came for the offering, those in the pews donated a whopping $22,700.

This initiative, which came to be called One Day to Feed the World, has since spread to hundreds of churches and businesses in America and around the globe. Even churches in Australia and China have caught the vision and have launched One Day to Feed the World in their nations. "The idea," says Jones, "is not to feed the world in a day—there is no way we'll ever be able to do that. But we can bring in one day's pay." It is a way to begin to take action against an escalating problem. Amazingly, the year that Alamo Christian Church launched the concept, its general fund grew by 21 percent, and its mission's fund grew by 42 percent! When people begin to give, they soon experience new joy and a sense of purpose. Giving begets giving.

Donate Goods

Whether you are interested in donating a truckload of potatoes, several pallets of granola bars, a pallet of mixed goods, assorted dairy products, or cases of soap or shampoo, these items and more can reach millions of hurting people through Convoy of Hope or your local food banks. Most organizations that collect and distribute what are called "Gifts in Kind" can transport dry, refrigerated, and frozen products of any quantity from their warehouses.

An unorganized local food drive can actually become a challenge for charitable organizations and your local food bank. To ensure the organization's high standards of quality and safety, the goods will need to be sorted and inspected. The best way to support hunger-relief is by making a financial donation to organizations like Convoy of Hope, Feeding America, Samaritan's Purse, or to your local food bank and admonishing your friends to do the same. This approach empowers the organization to cover transportation costs or, if need be, to purchase items at a discounted price.

Volunteer

There are many worthy organizations in which you can volunteer to serve in your own community and around the globe. Organizations such as Points of Light link volunteers to service opportunities. Convoy of Hope needs compassionate people to assist with community outreaches and disaster response. At our warehouses we need people to help sort, pack, count, label, and keep inventory. In addition, Convoy has an internship program with opportunities to serve for six weeks over the summer or three months in the spring or fall. Past interns have served in Central America, East Africa, North Asia, Eurasia, the Asia-Pacific, and all over the United States.

FROM DEPENDENCY TO SUSTAINABILITY

The biblical pattern clearly goes beyond simply meeting a needy person's immediate necessities. It charts a course that leads toward sustainability, toward the goal of empowering people to eventually meet their own needs. God provided manna for the Israelites during their desert wanderings, but His purpose was to sustain them as they marched toward a goal—the promised land (Ex. 16:31–35).

Once they got there, the heavenly manna stopped coming, and the people raised their own crops. We see this echoed in the story of Ruth. Ruth worked in Boaz's field and then was adopted into his household. It is interesting that one of the things that attracted Boaz to her was her work ethic.

Relief must be part of a continuum of care that leads a person and family to sustainability. Convoy of Hope feeds the hungry to meet their immediate need for food, but we also make sure to help individuals become self-sustainable through planting seed and managing their own gardens as well as training in nutrition and other life skills.

LEAVE NO CHILD OUTSIDE THE FENCE

On Tuesday, January 12, 2010, a 7.0 magnitude earthquake struck Haiti at a depth of 8.1 miles. The epicenter was located 15 miles off the coast of Port-au-Prince and killed at least three hundred thousand people and left one million Haitians homeless.[10] At the time, Convoy of Hope had an established distribution center in Haiti and was already feeding nine thousand children a day. A few months prior to the earthquake, I visited our feeding sites in Haiti, which are located in schools and orphanages where the children receive shelter, clothing, an education, and a nutritious meal each day.

Their only hope is that people like you will join the movement of hope and become relentless about making sure that no hungry child is left outside the fence.

While we were feeding the children I spotted out of the corner of my eye a young Haitian boy peering at us through the fence. I walked up to him and asked his name and he said, "Patrick."

Reaching out to shake his hand I said, "Nice to meet you Patrick, my name is Dave." Patrick shook my hand, but his gaze remained glued to the other children eating. "Are you hungry?" I asked. Patrick nodded his head. "When was the last time you ate?" He put up two fingers. "You have not eaten any food for two days?" He nodded his head again. I gave him a big grin and said, "Please come with me."

His face lit up as he crawled through the fence and followed me. As Patrick feasted on a delicious meal, other hungry children from the village gathered outside the fence hoping for the same invitation to enter the fenced area.

In response to the desperate need of children like Patrick, many generous and compassionate partners of Convoy of Hope donated the funds for Convoy to build a 36,000-square-foot distribution center in Haiti, which now provides nutritious meals each day for over fifty thousand children.

To children like Patrick, it's about you. Their only hope is that people like you will join the movement of hope and become relentless about making sure that no hungry child is left outside the fence.

CHAPTER 6 IN REVIEW

Key Ideas

1. Over 840 million people in the world are malnourished.

2. Over 200,000 children die each week due to malnourishment.

3. Approximately 3.5 percent of American households experience hunger.

4. It is estimated that the basic health and nutrition needs of the world's poorest poor could be met with the amount of money Americans and Europeans spend on pet food each year.

5. The biblical mandate to care for the poor extends beyond immediate needs and supports sustainability.

Discussion Questions

1. How can you help address the issue of global malnourishment?

2. The issue isn't the availability of resources; it is stewardship of the resources that are available. How can you and those you influence make a difference in the lives of the poor and needy in your community?

3. Global poverty is a problem, but domestic hunger is continuing to grow. Should the US spend money meeting the needs of other nations while Americans go hungry? Explain your response.

4. What lifestyle changes do you see the Relentless making in response to the worldwide hunger epidemic? What are some creative solutions you have seen or read about?

5. Is it easier to give a handout or teach people to care for their own needs? What is the best long-term solution?

Chapter 7

THIRTY JUMBO JETS HAVE CRASHED!

Imagine for a moment that you are relaxing at home and the phone rings. When you answer, you hear a friend's breathless voice: "Are you watching the news? Have you heard what has happened? It's horrible!" Grabbing the remote and turning on the television, you immediately discover that something earthshaking has taken place. Nearly every channel is being interrupted by a special report, so you flip over to your favorite news network.

The news anchor's expression is grim as he announces an unbelievable tragedy. During this one day, thirty jumbo jets have crashed, killing a total of 5,700 people. You are transfixed at the enormity of the catastrophe—thirty jumbo jets filled with passengers!

Of course, such a tragedy would keep news crews busy for many days and fill the front page headline in almost every newspaper. Every news network would lead its broadcast with the story and examine it from every angle. Commentators would analyze what went wrong and how it happened. Public officials and private citizens would pour out their expressions of grief and sorrow for the victims. Don't you think the whole world would be shocked and in mourning at the announcement of this awful event? Of course! Just to be clear, this event didn't happen; these thirty jets didn't crash. A more startling reality does exist though, and its magnitude is something like thirty jumbo jets crashing in the air. Only it's a lot more subtle than anyone might first realize. The number of children who will die today simply because they lack clean, safe water would fill all of these planes.

Water is central to human survival. We can live for weeks without food if we absolutely have to. But without water we can only survive for a matter of days. Water is life! The lack of access to adequate water contributes to deaths and illness, especially in children. According to WHO and UNICEF, more than three thousand children die each day from diarrheal diseases. Of these deaths 88 percent are due to poor drinking water, lack of sanitation, and poor hygiene.[1] Children under five represent 90 percent of all deaths caused by diarrheal diseases.[2]

In the Western world, we don't give much thought to water except when buying a bottle of water at a grocery store or from a convenient vending machine. For most of us, we simply turn on the faucet, and out comes as much water as we need. The typical American uses about sixty-nine gallons a day.[3] Also, according to the Washington Post in 2005, "Just one flush of a toilet in the West uses more water than most Africans have to perform an entire day's washing, cleaning, cooking, and drinking." If you have teenagers like me who take long showers, your number is probably higher! And in the average home, nearly ten gallons are simply wasted each day by leaky pipes and fittings.[4]

Use	Gallons per Capita	Percentage of Total Daily Use
Showers	11.6	16.8%
Clothes Washers	15.0	21.7%
Dishwashers	1.0	1.4%

Use	Gallons per Capita	Percentage of Total Daily Use
Toilets	18.5	26.7%
Baths	1.2	1.7%
Leaks	9.5	13.7%
Faucets	10.9	15.7%
Other Domestic Use	1.6	2.2%

What if you had to carry nearly 70 gallons of water every day from a water source to your home? Let's do the math: 1 gallon of water weighs approximately 8.32 pounds, so 69.3 gallons equals more than 576 pounds. Think about the impossibility of carrying 576 pounds of water from a lake or stream to your home each and every day.

In most third world countries, women and children usually retrieve the water. If the average person could carry twenty pounds of water, she would have to make twenty-nine trips. Of course, the poor are using only a fraction of the amount of water that we Americans use, but much of their lives are consumed with trying to gather enough water to survive.

DYING FOR WATER

During droughts, I have experienced the horror of seeing people who have died from the rigors of searching for water. One missionary told me that over a period of time, when they get less and less rain, people's capacity to rebound is lowered, and they finally die or just give up. I can't forget the sight of an elderly woman lying dead alongside a road with a container in her hand. She was fetching water for her family, but the weight and distance were finally too much for her frail body.

If the weight and rigor of transporting the water doesn't get to you, it is likely criminals might. It is all too common for women to be attacked and raped while traveling away from the security of their village to fetch water for their family. This nightmare, played out every day for millions, does not need to happen! We have the technology to establish wells and water systems in villages and communities wherever there is need.

In addition to the danger of journeying to find water, people unknowingly draw from water sources that are not clean and safe. Tainted water transports all kinds of deadly germs and bacteria and is responsible for an unbelievable number of deaths every day. UNICEF estimates that 1.1 billion people in the world have no access to safe drinking water and that 2.2 million people—most of them children—die

> { We have the technology to establish wells and water systems in villages and communities wherever there is need. }

each year from lack of access to safe drinking water and adequate sanitation.[5] The result is a plethora of diseases. A UNICEF report states, "more than 150 million school-age children are severely affected by waterborne parasites like roundworm, whipworm, and hookworm. These children commonly carry up to 1,000 parasites at a time, causing anemia, stunted growth, and other debilitating conditions."[6] These health conditions also affect the ability of students to perform well in school and undermine their chances to get ahead. More than half of all schools worldwide lack safe water and sanitation. We have seen the effects of cholera in Haiti, which is caused by drinking contaminated water.

It is time to wake up to an international crisis much bigger than any tsunami or hurricane could ever be. Half of the world's hospital beds are filled with people suffering from water-related illnesses. More than a billion people are without safe drinking water worldwide, and a child dies every twenty seconds from water-related diseases. At any one time, patients suffering from waterborne diseases occupy half of the world's hospital beds.[7]

WATER SOLUTIONS

The good news is that we have the ability to help many of these villages combat droughts and prevent water-related disease through proven water interventions. Here are three examples of what can be done, simply and effectively.

1. We can help drill wells to tap into water sources deep in the earth.

Many people die trying to dig their own wells. Lowered by ropes, they dig by hand, only to have the walls cave in on them. Others have died from methane gases in the wells. And even when people find water, they have no guarantee it will be fit for consumption.

The Oasis Project, Water for the World, and WorldServe are leading organizations seeking to provide safe and accessible water throughout the African continent. They have many success stories, like the village of Mwanabaya in Tanzania, a village of two thousand inhabitants, whose lives were drastically improved after a well was dug for them by Oasis Project. Now, instead of walking miles to retrieve potentially dangerous water, the townspeople of Mwanabaya can bring their buckets to the town pump and get all they need.

2. We can provide water purification packets.

In communities where we can't drill a well, we can help harvest water with guttering cisterns and then make sure it's clean and safe to drink by using purification packets. These little packets, about half the size of a credit card, are filled with a chemical powder that kills harmful bacteria and viruses. Within thirty minutes, previously unsafe water is crystal clear and safe to drink. Millions of these packets have already been distributed throughout the world in impoverished or disaster-ravaged areas.

3. We can set up two types of water filtration systems.

One system uses the Sawyer filters, which use the same technology as dialysis. A small spigot and hose are attached to a five-gallon bucket that can offer hundreds of gallons of purified water each day. The maintenance is minimal. The other system is bio-sand filtration units that use local materials to filter the water. With no filters to change, there is no upkeep cost to these units. Each system can provide enough clean water for an entire family to have safe water every day.

ECONOMIC CENTS

I have worked in Washington, D.C. for over a decade and can't comprehend why some members of Congress refuse to acknowledge that spending funds on water solutions, sanitation, food, health prevention, and education on AIDS prevention in the developing world actually saves billions of dollars in the long-term. Some argue that cuts in government spending is the way to resolve budget deficits and, with so many Americans unemployed, the government can no longer afford to provide foreign assistance. The fact is, foreign assistance is only 1.1 percent of the total United States budget and, if invested correctly, will prevent death and disease and reduce the expense for future generations.[8]

In a Facebook article in April of 2011, Jim Thebaut wrote, "It is projected that by 2050 the earth's population could be as high as 9.2 billion and there will not be enough food or water to sustain the world. This perilous situation could set the stage for global wars and nuclear proliferation, which would obviously profoundly threaten US national security. Foreign assistance can help to divert this impending, potential global calamity. In addition, it's regrettable that the media doesn't focus some significant journalism on this issue as well as hold Congress accountable for this critical shortcoming!"[9]

Having visited many of the USAID Mission offices, there is no question that some requests for refunding have been denied due to the corruption of leaders in the developing world and the lack of assurance that funds will make it to their intended purpose. In fairness, some foreign leaders say they have refused US support because they view the assistance with strings attached. These foreign leaders fear that they will be pressured into becoming a more democratic society with special attention paid to human and civil rights.

In his article, Thebaut continues, "United States funding in the future should require significantly more accountability and scrutiny to assure that foreign assistance programs are more effective. The aid recipients should also be strategically globally targeted in order to save maximum lives (particularly children's), stimulate economic development, counter terrorism and sex and drug trafficking. In addition, there should be an emphasis towards targeting strategic public/private partners for additional funding and in-kind geopolitical support. The overall objective is to bring governments, the private sector, academia and non-governmental organizations together throughout the world in order to implement sustainable solutions and, most importantly, save lives."[10]

IT WAS A CELEBRATION!

When I first met Wachira Karani, he impressed me with his humility and his dream of helping children throughout Kenya, Somalia, and Ethiopia. His smile gave way to a determined expression. Wachira explained, "I was an orphan living on the streets and left to die when someone rescued me. I have got to save these children before they die of hunger or disease or waste away sniffing glue." As a pastor, he had already planted forty-three churches, including his own, which more than seven hundred people attend. The church grounds include a school and a group home for orphans.

I stood with Wachira on a barren piece of land that his church had purchased, and he pointed in multiple directions, showing me where he planned to locate a school that would hold 1,500 children. "Over there we will build another group home for orphans, and over there a farm and stalls for livestock." Then without warning, he bent to his knees and pointed straight down to the ground and said, "Mr. Dave, I can do all of this if I just had a well right here to supply us with water."

I knelt down beside him and made eye contact. "Pastor, Convoy of Hope will raise the funds to drill this well." We hugged and prayed that God would bring a spring of resources for this worthy project. I returned home and contacted a few pastor friends and all of the funds for the well and water pump were raised.

News of the project spread throughout Wachira's community. When the rig arrived to drill for water, so did the crowds. People looked on with anticipation, praying that life-giving water would spring forth. For hours, the rig carved through the compacted dirt in a quest to discover the world's most precious resource. Then, at 164 meters, the miracle of life happened as the drilling unit met a wonderful underground riverbed and out came clean, fresh water. The people shouted with joy, sang songs, and praised God for the gift of life He had brought to the community through water.

A few months later Pastor Karani and I stood together at the site of the new well. His eyes glistened with excitement as he recalled, "Brother Dave, I wish you could have been here as the water was gushing out of the ground. People arrived from everywhere with plastic containers. The line of people was all the way down the street! It was a great celebration, and I thank God that my dream for this community is coming true!"

CHAPTER 7 IN REVIEW

Key Ideas

1. The typical American family uses sixty-nine gallons of water per day with ten gallons per day wasted through leaks in plumbing systems.

2. UNICEF estimates that 400 million children have no access to safe drinking water.

3. Worldwide, a child dies every fifteen seconds from water-related diseases.

4. Many organizations are working hard to improve the availability of safe drinking water.

5. An investment of 1.1 percent of the annual budget of the United States could prevent disease and death in future generations.

Discussion Questions

1. What are some ways you can conserve the natural resources that are so readily available?

2. What is your reaction to the fact that 400 million children have no access to clean water?

3. Do an Internet search for organizations that are working to provide clean water. What can you do to help support these efforts?

4. Water is a localized resource; it generally requires organizations to drill wells and provide filtration and purification. How does our conservation of resources affect the availability of similar resources in other parts of the world?

5. What is your plan of action in response to knowing about the global tragedy that is affecting so many innocent people?

Chapter 8

PLEASE
TAKE MY BABY!

As we made our way through Calcutta's Victoria Square, our driver spotted a street vendor offering cold drinks. The heat had been oppressive all morning, and we were all thirsty. Finding a place to pull off, he got out of the car and made his way to the vendor to get us each a Coke while we remained in the car with our windows rolled down.

I sat there taking in the rush and bustle of crowds of people scrambling through the market area. Some were shopping, some were hawking their goods, and some were begging for food or money. My arm was hanging out the window, and my eyes drifted through the crowd.

Suddenly, I felt a sharp tug at my sleeve. Turning my head, I met the eyes of a young Indian woman who was pleading with me in Hindi while hoisting her crying baby towards my open window. I fumbled in my pocket for a few coins and handed them to her, thinking she needed money to buy food for her child and that would be the end to our encounter. But, to my dismay, she waved off the money and pleaded louder and louder while thrusting her baby in my direction. My immediate thought was she wanted more money than what I had offered. Frustrated by her ingratitude, I began to roll up my window.

By that time, the driver had returned. He had watched the whole episode unfold. After he got into the car, he turned to me and said, "She is not wanting your money. She is pleading with you to take her baby." My heart sank to the floor.

"Do you mean she wants me to take her child home with me to America?" The driver nodded his head and said, "Yes. She believes her baby will die if you do not take him." I glanced quickly at the desperate woman's eyes, which will be branded on my heart until my last breath. Overwhelmed by the moment, I cowardly fished out my sunglasses to shield my eyes and ducked below the dashboard to escape this woman's living nightmare.

WHO WILL GET TO THEM FIRST?

Violence, exploitations, and abuse are widespread among children in developing countries, especially for children living outside households, such as children living or working on the streets and children living in institutions. While these children often represent a minority, their living arrangements may put them at increased risk of exploitation or abuse.[1] In many developing countries, an average of 18 percent of girls ages fifteen to nineteen years old report they have experienced sexual violence. One in six children, ages five to fourteen is engaged in child labor.[2]

The need is urgent. Every day, every minute, precious young lives are slipping away. The race is not only for the survival of these children but also for their rescue before they are recruited by warlords and terrorists. Radical groups like Al Qaeda find an inexhaustible supply of children and youth among orphans to help them carry on their campaigns of terror. The images of small boys carrying automatic weapons and artillery are some of the most disturbing of our time. These boys are recruited into militias, where they get their primary needs met, receive recognition, and find a sense of purpose in exchange for becoming young killing machines.

I have personally interviewed young girls who are pressed into service as prostitutes to serve the sexual desires of soldiers and tourists. Sitting next to a middle-aged man on a plane, he conceded, "There are now organized trips for men to visit cities for the sake of having sex with as many virgins as possible." It seems a tragedy beyond comprehension, yet tens of thousands of children are used as human shields in conflicts around the world. In the city of Sderot, located just tmiles from Gaza, the residents are awakened many mornings with alarms of incoming missiles. It broke my heart when an official from Israel's government showed me schools and playgrounds for kids that are hidden deep inside huge fortified bunkers.

> The race is not only for the survival of these children but also for their rescue before they are recruited by warlords and terrorists.

FOSTER CARE—
AMERICA'S LIVING GRAVEYARD

In America, over 500,000 children are in the foster care system, which one social worker called, "a virtual graveyard" for these kids.[3] For the fortunate, foster children finding a home where they will not be sexually or verbally abused is a victory. One adult who had been passed from home to home for over fifteen years told me, "Most of us realize that the foster parents really do not want us, but if it means that the government will give them enough to make their truck payment then the trade-off is worth it." Our foster daughter confided that at a previous home it was understood that she was welcome as long as she stayed out of everybody's way. She learned quickly that the best way to do that was to spend most days alone in her room.

Make no mistake about it; these children will not remain in limbo while we make up our minds. Their futures are being determined every day that passes.

GOD'S SHORT LIST

James, the half brother of Jesus, stated in his letter that caring for orphans is actually part of the definition of genuine faith approved by God: "Religion that God our Father accepts as pure and faultless is this: to look after orphans and widows in their distress and to keep oneself from being polluted by the world" (James 1:27). This passage should become an annoying popup on our computer screen reminding us of the importance God's places on rescuing and serving orphans.

If you are contemplating your priorities as a person, family, church, charity, or business, I challenge you to listen to God's plea through James 1:27. When envisioning a bigger and more beautiful edifice, employing more staff, or expanding your programs and planning budgets, would you consider making outreach to orphans the centerpiece of your mission? Where else in the Bible is it made so clear what kind of faith in action is pleasing to God?

Join me as we take closer look at the plight of orphans in underdeveloped countries and in the United States and discover what we can do.

ORPHANS—LIVING IN UNDERDEVELOPED COUNTRIES

Most of the children living in underdeveloped countries face four potential futures: death from hunger and disease, forced prostitution, conscription by evil dictators and warlords, or rescue—being fed, clothed, and educated so they can be part of bringing about change among their own people. Failing to reach these children ensures the continuation of the devastating cycle of despair.

The good news for these orphans is that they are many examples of models of hope that we can support such as the Kenya Kids Home in Nairobi, Kenya.

THE HOPE EXPERIENCE

The Kenya Kids Home is one of the finest models in the world for rescuing, restoring, and training orphans to becoming productive citizens and agents of hope for their nation. The Home staff take care of about eighty children at a time, most of them for at least one year. During their time in the Home, the children receive counseling and attend informal schooling, which prepares them for later entry into public schools. They also learn about God's love, sing in a choir, memorize Scripture, and develop basic life skills, such as proper hygiene and good manners.

After one year, the children are transferred, ten or twelve at a time, to a group home that is sustained by a local church and where a couple assigned by the pastor become the children's adoptive parents. This group home of ten to twelve children becomes a closely-knit African family where nurturing and development occur in a warm and safe environment.

Convoy of Hope takes business leaders and pastors on vision trips to Africa, Latin America, and Haiti where they can experience the squalor of poverty and the splendor of seeing how they can make a difference. We call these vision trips The Hope Experience. Again and again, I have seen how these experiences change people, how they motivate folks to get involved when they see that poverty has a name, a face, and a pair of eyes looking back at them. Following his Hope Experience to Kenya, Michael Kern, president and COO of Stout Risius Ross, shared this reflection: "As our team journeyed through Kenya's Mathare Valley—one of the world's poorest communities—I saw, heard, smelled, felt, and experienced things that destroyed the barriers separating my isolated world from the impoverished one I was walking through. It's one thing to hear about hungry children; it's another to look them in the eyes. Though I knew beforehand that I would encounter all these things, I never expected my life, goals, ambitions, dreams, and heart to be so utterly transformed by what I experienced."

You can learn more about Hope Experience trips by going to www.convoyofhope.org.

IS THIS WHAT THEY CALL HEAVEN?

The founder of Kenya Kids Home is Peter Njiri. Every day he comes face-to-face with the heart wrenching realities of how lives are destroyed by need and deprivation. One evening, the program director opened the front door of the orphanage and discovered a filthy, battered, and dangerously malnourished little boy who had been abandoned on his steps. Perhaps desperate parents had left him there because they had run out of options and could no longer feed and look after him. The little boy was very weak and frail. Realizing that the young lad could barely stand up, the director scooped him up and carried him inside. He placed him in a bed amidst several rows of bunk beds. Pulling back the covers, the director slipped the boy's fragile, bony legs underneath and tenderly assured the frightened boy, "We do not know who left you on our doorstep, but you are safe here. We will take care of you." He kissed the boy on the forehead and repeated, "You are safe now. Go to sleep."

During bed checks later that night, the director was startled to see the boy's bed empty. He and his staff searched for the missing child. When they found him, he was not outside and had not run away. In the darkness, they had overlooked him hiding on the floor under the bed.

The director picked him up and tucked him back in the covers. "Why were you sleeping on the floor?" he asked. "I have never slept in a bed," the boy answered quietly. Then, with tears filling his scared but hopeful eyes, he asked, "Is this what they call heaven?"

WANTED: IMPERFECT FOSTER PARENTS

A director for a foster care agency in Northern Virginia told me, "I see these beautiful kids enter foster care because they have been abused and neglected. For example, we had a boy who slept underneath his bed in the foster home for six months because that is where he slept in his birth home. It was the safest place for him with all of the domestic violence that went on all hours of the day and night. We discovered an eleven-year-old who was pregnant with her mom's boyfriend's baby. We had three kids who had never been out of their home in their life."

It is painful to think what these kids have been through. When I asked the director why people should consider becoming foster parents, he replied, "To change the world one child at a time." He believes this is a powerful ministry that the whole church should embrace. Relentless followers of Jesus should be taking the lead when it comes to protecting and caring for these children.

Across the nation, I have talked with many followers of Jesus who would like to become foster parents but have never taken that step because of fear of failure and the unknown. There are over 300,000 churches in America. If just one family from each church became a foster parent or Forever Family for one of the 133,000 children who have been approved for adoption, we could make a significant impact quickly. Some prospective parents for these children abandon the idea when they buy the excuses of "being too busy" or not being able to provide a perfect situation. But perfection is not what these kids need. They need imperfect parents with love to give.

A few years ago, the US Children's Bureau produced several very creative commercials to recruit foster and adoptive parents. Their theme was "You don't have to be perfect to be a perfect parent." One of my favorites in this series opens with a father and son playing musical instruments in their garage. The boy is on the drums and the dad is trying to play the saxophone. A close-up shows the boy grimacing as his dad squeaks up and down the scale, trying to find the right key. Then both the father and son glance at each other, smiling ear to ear, as you hear the voiceover, "You don't have to be perfect to be a perfect parent."

> If just one family from each church became a foster parent or Forever Family for one of the 133,000 children who have been approved for adoption, we could make a significant impact quickly.

Another commercial begins with two boys playing basketball outside their home. One boy shoots the ball, and it gets stuck between the rim and the backboard. The two boys moan as they stare up at the ball, thinking that their game is ruined. Just then a mom enters the scene carrying a broom. She points the handle toward the basketball and dislodges it, much to the boys' glee. Again you hear the voiceover, "You don't have to be perfect to be a perfect parent." What these children need most is simply the presence of a caring adult. And as someone once told me, love is spelled T-I-M-E.

Focus on the Family has been at the vanguard in raising the awareness of the plight of orphans worldwide and challenging Christians to become Forever Families to these children. You can read more about what they do at the Web site www. iCareAboutOrphans.org. As foster parents, my wife and I can attest that it isn't always easy or convenient. However, having been both foster and adoptive parents we will be the first to testify how making room in your life for these kids will bless your marriage, your family, and your home. You will be enriched by practicing "pure religion" that pleases God (James 1:27).

GOD'S RISKY PROMISE TO ORPHANS

God made a promise that He would be "a father to the fatherless" (Ps. 68:5). It is a promise to the fatherless that He is relentless in keeping. However, God is in a fix because He has limited Himself to just one option if His promise is to be fulfilled. Why would He make such a promise and then risk it all on one, unpredictable option?

He must be so confident in that option that no backup plans are needed. So what is the solution to fulfilling His promise to the fatherless? The answer is set in the next verse, "God sets the lonely in families"(Ps. 68:6). Think about it! God is so confident that you and I will invite the fatherless into our families that He boldly promises it to the orphans and to the world.

Job, the biblical character who learned to trust in God through suffering, understood God's promise to orphans and His expectation for us to share our homes with them. He made it the passion of His life: "Whoever heard me spoke well of me, and those who saw me commended me, because I rescued the poor who cried for help, and the fatherless who had none to assist him. . . . I was a father to the needy; I took up the case of the stranger. I broke the fangs of the wicked and snatched the victims from their teeth" (Job 29:11–12,16–17).

Are you prepared, like Job, to help snatch the world's orphans from the jaws of hunger, violence, abuse, forced prostitution, and despair? Are you willing to stop making excuses and accept the fact that God is counting on you to keep His promise to an orphan child? Are you ready to open the door to your heart and home and to become an imperfect parent to the child God yearns to set in your family?

CHAPTER 8 IN REVIEW

Key Ideas

1. Worldwide there are over 150 million children living on the streets.

2. Radical militant groups prey on desperate children by recruiting them to serve their hate-based causes.

3. In America, over a half million children are in the foster care system.

4. Most of the children in third world countries face four potential futures: death from hunger and disease, forced prostitution, conscription by evil warlords and dictators, or rescue.

5. There are over 300,000 churches in America. If one family in each church became foster parents, the 133,000 children who have been approved for adoption would have permanent homes.

Discussion Questions

1. Where in your community are the needs of homeless children and families being met? What can you do to partner with those organizations?

2. What would happen to radical militant groups if the number of homeless children worldwide was reduced?

3. What can you do to provide care and support for kids in the foster care system?

4. Review the four potential futures of children in need. Three of those futures become reality when we do nothing. Why is doing nothing not an option? Why is it so easy for Americans to do nothing?

5. Does your church have a ministry for foster families? If so, what can you do to support it? If not, what can you do to help start one?

Chapter 9

AMERICA'S HIDDEN OUTCASTS

D o you know my name?" He asked as he stood before me with a weather-beaten face, matted hair, a toothless grin, and a smell that attacked all of my senses.

Moments earlier I had challenged others through a sermon to look for opportunities to reach out to the untouchables. My challenge from the pulpit was followed by a light chorus of "Amen" that echoed from the crowd. After passing the microphone to the host pastor, I slipped down the aisle to station myself at the doors of the foyer in order to greet people as they left. In my haste, I rushed right past a little cluster of homeless men who had come in off the street to get a pre-service meal and to sit (or should I say, mostly sleep) through the service.

As the pastor's closing prayer continued, the restroom door suddenly opened behind me, and a homeless man shuffled out into the foyer. He looked ragged and dirty. His body odor cast an unwelcome cloud. I glanced in his direction and then back toward the front of the church hoping to escape his approach.

"Do you know my name?" I turned again, wondering whom he

was speaking to. When our eyes met, I saw that he was talking to me. He approached me and repeated his question. With searching eyes I replied, "I'm sorry, but I don't know your name."

"My name," he said firmly and with a hint of pride, "is Joe." "Hi Joe, my name is Dave. Nice to meet you." I hoped that would end our exchange and aid my retreat. "You probably think I only come here to get food, don't you?" Before I could respond he continued, "Dave, I am grateful for the food, but I come here for only one reason." His eyes now filling with tears, "I want someone to remember my name."

Are we willing to admit that people like Joe are less than fully human figures whom we avoid as we go to the office, school, or church? Jesus never made that mistake. In the parable of the sheep and the goats, Jesus spoke of helping those without food, water, clothing, and shelter. He said, "Whatever you did for one of the least of these brothers of mine, you did for me" (Matt. 25:40).

As Jesus unfolded this story, He consistently used personal pronouns—you, my, and me. To Jesus, poverty was personal and relational. Perhaps that's why we feel closest to Jesus when we're with the poor. To Jesus, poverty always had a name, a face, and an unfathomable value.

RELENTLESS FOR SOCIAL OUTCASTS

The Gospels record a number of occasions when Jesus healed people who suffered from leprosy, a highly infectious disease that disfigures and wastes away the flesh. You don't hear much about that disease today, at least not in America thanks to advances in our medical research and practice. But this is still a terrible plight for poor people around the world.

In the ancient world, this disease was believed to be so contagious, in fact, that its victims were quarantined in remote places in order to separate them from others who might get infected (Lev. 13:45–46). You might say those who suffered from this terrible disease were victims twice over—they were both physically impaired and socially isolated. But while others avoided the lepers at all costs, Jesus reached out to them—literally. He not only allowed them to approach Him but also touched them, laying hands on them in order to heal them (Mark 1:40–42).

THE "EXPENDABLE ELDERLY"

Leprosy is no longer common, but the way we quarantine some of the poor in America is tragically similar. Today, the most populous but hidden outcasts are the elderly, homeless families, and run-away youth.

The elderly are most often neglected, abandoned, and left to die alone. Currently, 3.5 million Americans age sixty-five and older live below the poverty line.[1] They once served and waited on us, but now many are shut-ins, stowed away in nursing homes and seldom visited by their loved ones. These are men and women who worked hard all their lives. They are someone's father, mother, brother, sister, or child.

Often their life savings are quickly erased by family problems or a major medical emergency or some other unforeseen expense. Among these are veterans who sacrificed a great deal while fighting for their country in World War II, Korea, or Vietnam. They sacrificed so their children could have comfort and safety, a good education, and a better life than they had. But now, in their latter years, they find themselves broke and dependent on Social Security benefits, which are not really adequate to make ends meet. Their challenges are too big and too disruptive to our lifestyles so we forget about them or hide from them. They are often treated as if they are expendable!

On a visit to a doctor's office for a routine checkup, I sat down next to a kind elderly couple and struck up a conversation. They looked tired, so I asked them how long they had been waiting. They told me about two hours. Not long after that, the front desk clerk called my name. As I approached the desk, I said, "That couple over there has been waiting for two hours, and I have only been here for about thirty minutes. Why am I getting to go ahead of them even though they have waited so much longer?"

She glanced in their direction and gave me a knowing smile, "Don't worry about it. They have time." Attempting to control my anger I asked, "Do you believe it is right to decide that their time is less important than mine just because I am younger?" Then I walked back to my seat and said to the couple, "The clerk was mistaken, you are next."

Our society sometimes seems to operate on the proposition that if you are not of value to me, then you are expendable. Until we begin to appreciate the legacy a previous generation has left to us and accept responsibility to make sure its members receive good care and are

> Our society sometimes seems to operate on the proposition that if you are not of value to me, then you are expendable.

treated with dignity, we have failed. The good news for the elderly is that there are effective models of hope for them as described below in both church-based and for-profit sectors:

Florence Gardens

Florence Gardens is the senior living community of Canyon Hills Church in Bakersfield, California. Florence Gardens was developed in response to our scriptural mandate to care for the seniors of both our church and community. Each day Florence Gardens serves as a hub for ministry and care to the seniors who live in one of the one hundred homes on campus or who come to the center simply to participate in the myriad of activities, groups, or Bible studies in the clubhouse or other activity environments of the community.

SeniorCorp

SeniorCorp was established in 2003 to address the need in the community for compassionate, quality in-home care services for the aging population. Tom Knox recognized a gap in care services for the elderly after his own experiences with his aging grandparents. His paternal grandmother, Edith, suffered from Alzheimer's disease and was in and out of assisting living, forcing his grandparents to spend all of their resources to qualify for Medicaid.

Tom was determined to change the way America ages. Senior-Corp now offers seniors the ability to remain in their homes as they age, where they can still feel comfortable, safe, and happy. Senior-Corp companions are well-trained to provide assisted-living services such as light housekeeping, laundry, organizing mail, entertainment, transportation, personal care, meal planning, and more—all done with a smile, love, and support.

THE FORGOTTEN FAMILIES

When you hear the word *homeless*, what picture comes into your mind? If you are like most people, you'll probably imagine someone like Joe, a scruffy bearded man who smells bad and stands on the street corner with a sign, trying to get money that you suspect he will use to buy liquor. Or maybe you think of a young drug addict who sleeps curled up on a park bench and shoplifts to feed his habit.

Or perhaps it is a middle-aged woman with a wild and frightening look in her eyes who mutters nonsense and occasionally yells obscenities at passers-by.

We tend to think of the homeless in this way because this is the segment of the homeless population that is most visible and most unavoidable as we go about our daily activities. If this is your impression of homelessness, you are not alone. But the largely hidden segment of the homeless population is made up of families. The shocking truth is that families with young children account for an appalling 41 percent of the nation's homeless.[2] That is a 23 percent increase from 2007.

A majority of homeless people counted were in emergency shelters or transitional housing programs, but nearly four in ten were unsheltered, living on the streets, or in cars, abandoned buildings, or other places not intended for human habitation. The unsheltered population increased by 2 percent from 239,759 in 2009 to 243,701 in 2011, the only subpopulation to increase.

The "doubled up" population (people who live with friends, family or other nonrelatives for economic reasons) increased by 13 percent from 6 million in 2009 to 6.8 million in 2010. The doubled up population increased by more than 50 percent from 2005 to 2010.[3]

These families are largely hidden out of sight—sleeping in their cars, abandoned buildings, emergency shelters, or substandard hotels. They don't draw much attention to themselves, and they often try to retain their dignity and some small sense of normalcy for their children. They scrape, save, and sacrifice, but they can't seem to get ahead. They float from location to location, looking for work of any sort, and their children's educational development is disrupted by their nomadic lifestyle.

Those who may suffer most in the wake of this vagabond

existence are the children, emotionally bruised from the trauma of roving from place to place and the embarrassment of not having someplace to come home to. They grow up with little security, and in spite of their resilience, these kids tend to show visible signs of their stressful lifestyle, such as depression, deep-seated fears, anxiety, and even high blood pressure. If they are able to attend school, they usually perform below average.

I have met a lot of these kids at various Convoy of Hope outreaches and can usually spot them by their unkempt appearance, worn-out countenance, and social backwardness. They desire a normal life more than anything, but many of them have lost hope. At one of Convoy's December outreaches, I asked a young homeless boy what he wanted for Christmas. He just looked up at me with weary yet hopeful eyes and said, "To stay in a home."

Many situations can render a family homeless. Sometimes the family unit is fractured, and the primary breadwinner may disappear. Other times, substance abuse drains the family economy of what little money they might otherwise have. Sometimes parents lack the life skills needed to find and sustain a job. At other times, catastrophe strikes. Families may be displaced by natural disasters, such as devastating floods, hurricanes, and fires. The money-earning member of the family may die, or that person's job may fall victim to a struggling economy.

The global economic crisis and the resulting foreclosures and high unemployment dropped many from the middle class into a desperate fight for survival. A record number of families now living on food stamps belies the usual stereotypes of the impoverished and homeless. There are over three million homeless in America, and an additional five million poor who spend more than half of their income on housing, leaving them always just on the cusp of homelessness.[4] They would be quick to tell you that with one missed paycheck or a major medical emergency, the mounting bills would push them over the edge and onto the streets. Dispirited government officials and church leaders who never dreamed this would become the plight of their American neighbors are accepting this as the "new normal."

ON THE RUN

As you widen the aperture for hidden outcasts, you uncover the high number of young people ages sixteen to twenty-four who are on the run. They may comprise as much as 12 percent of the homeless population. Many of these are kids who have fled from home or have been thrown out by their parents. Fueling the upward trend of homeless youth is the disturbing number of high school dropouts. One teen drops out of school every twenty-six seconds which is 7,200 kids every day.[5] There is no people group in America more hidden and at risk than homeless youth.

> There is no people group in America more hidden and at risk than homeless youth.

PROBLEMS OR OPPORTUNITIES

Sitting on the church platform, I patiently waited for the pastor to introduce me to speak. He awkwardly leaned over the podium and then nervously cleared his throat before dropping a bombshell on the church and this guest speaker. The pastor said, "I had not planned to announce this today but my wife and I believe our time as your pastor has come to an end. This morning we submitted our resignation to the church board."

Then without any delay he introduced me to speak. Adding to the drama my sermon topic was, "Never Quit!" After the service the pastor confided in me that the reason he was leaving was because he believed there are too many problems in his community.

What a blinded view! What this pastor saw as problems God sees as opportunity for the church to bring hope and healing. I said to this pastor, "God has placed in this church and community more than enough assets to meet every spiritual, emotional, and physical need."

THE "WALMART CHURCH"

In 1858, Rowland Macy had a fresh new idea. He realized that people often spent hours—maybe even a full day—shopping for their various necessities. They would visit a clothing store for clothing, a grocery store for food, a dry-goods store for fabrics and supplies, a furniture store for furniture, a haberdashery for hats, and so on. He wondered what would happen if someone built one huge store that carried all these items and more. Could this store become a one-stop destination and meet most of the needs that consumers have? With this vision in mind, Macy built the world's first department store in New York City. It had several floors of merchandise—almost anything a person could want and need. And it was all in one place! Of course, it was a raging success and it forever changed the way people think about shopping.[6] In our own time, stores like Walmart have expanded upon this model with huge success.

Might our churches learn something from this model? Might we develop churches where people can go to see all of their needs met? Where the church can respond to people's needs of all kinds—whether spiritual, emotional, relational, or physical?

The good news for America's outcasts is that the number of these "Walmart" churches is growing, and they are becoming epicenters for spiritual and social renewal in their communities.

There are two Walmart type churches I'd like to highlight: One is First Assembly of God in Concord, North Carolina. Pastor Rick Ross likes to say, "Concord First Assembly is a church that desires to love God, love people, and pass it on. No matter your age, interests, or where you are on your spiritual journey, we have something for everyone." You can learn more about this church by visiting www.cfaconcord.com.

Pastor Wendell Vinson, at Canyon Hills Church in Bakersfield, California, developed "The Adventure," which offers a menu of programs that connect people to the life-flow of the church and empowers them to serve God with greater purpose and passion. Take time to learn more about these terrific programs at www.canyonhills.com. Both of these churches are what I call "one stop shops," where people can find a family atmosphere of love and acceptance and programs to help them grow spiritually, relationally, emotionally, and financially.

Why is this Walmart model of church important for our world today? "When asked to give the important factors used when selecting a church to visit, 66 percent of un-churched people surveyed said 'How much the people in the church seem to care about each other' was extremely important or very important to them. Sixty percent of un-churched people surveyed said 'How much the church is involved in helping the poor and disadvantaged' was extremely important or very important to them."[7]

HABITAT FOR HUMANITY

For homeless families, temporary housing such as shelters should be just that—temporary. People need a better long-term solution. One organization at the forefront of working with local churches and community groups to provide affordable homes is Habitat for Humanity International (HFHI). In 1976, Millard and Linda Fuller founded this Christian organization to help provide quality homes for those in need. Now, more than thirty years later, several hundred thousand homes have been built around the world, providing millions of people with safe, affordable, good-quality housing.

Here is an interview I conducted with Jonathan Reckford, CEO of HFHI, about what they do, why they do it and how to get involved:

Dave: Why are you personally involved in providing shelter?

Jonathan: I was drawn to Habitat for two important reasons. First, I believe that a safe, decent, and affordable home is the foundation for a better life for every family. Second, the way Habitat engages volunteers to partner with families in need transforms everyone involved in the process. Because families put in sweat equity and pay an affordable no-profit mortgage, they are given the chance to pull themselves up. I had the chance to see that transformation firsthand as a volunteer back in the early '90s and have been a fan of Habitat ever since. Extensive data indicate that stable, affordable housing is central to education, health, employment, and economic development.

Dave: What is the mission of HFHI?

Jonathan: As a Christian housing ministry, the mission of HFHI is to eliminate poverty housing and homelessness from the face of the earth by building adequate and basic housing. We partner with people of all backgrounds, races, and religions to build houses together in partnership with families in need, and we seek to put shelter on the hearts and minds of people in such a powerful way that poverty housing and homelessness become socially, politically, and religiously unacceptable in our world.

Dave: How does it work? How do you partner with the community and the family to secure the land, build the home, and then pay for it?

Jonathan: Through volunteer labor and donations of money and materials, Habitat builds and rehabilitates simple, decent houses alongside home-owner (partner) families. Families in need of decent shelter apply to local Habitat groups called affiliates. The affiliate's family selection committee chooses home owners based on their level of need, their willingness to become partners in the program, and their ability to repay the loan. Every affiliate follows a nondiscriminatory policy of family selection. Habitat is not a giveaway program. In addition to a down payment and monthly mortgage payments, homeowners invest hundreds of hours of their own labor into building their Habitat house and the houses of others. Habitat houses are sold to partner families at no profit and financed with affordable loans. The homeowners' monthly mortgage payments are used to build more Habitat houses.

Dave: Why is it important to build collaborations around providing shelter for the poor? What is your strategy?

Jonathan: HFHI cannot be the sole answer to the problem of affordable housing around the world. It is going to take many partners working together on a large scale and in local communities to develop housing solutions. Together, we can accomplish more than each of us can do alone.

Dave: How can someone volunteer to participate in Habitat for Humanity?

Jonathan: Much of our work is done through local groups called affiliates. Using the search engine on our website, www. habitat.org, you can locate the affiliate nearest you and talk with the leaders there about volunteering to build or repair a home, about serving on a committee, about donating funds or services, or advocating for just housing policy and more.

THE DREAM HOME

Let me close with the story of one homeless boy and how a church reached out to his family. Prior to his untimely death, the father of this young boy had purchased a fixer-upper home in one city and a vacant lot at the end of a dirt road in a nearby town. While they were working out the details of moving and remodeling their dream home, the family was living in a cheap hotel room.

> The tragic death of a father and husband who had planned to build a dream home for his family was fulfilled by Christians who put feet to their faith and action to their convictions.

One night, a reckless car skidded across a divide and collided with the father's car. The father was killed, and the dream of a home for his family appeared likely to die as well. Without any resources, the family was poised to lose both the home and the property.

In the meantime, the family was functionally homeless. But those close to the deceased father knew how much he loved that home and had dreamed of it sitting on that barren land he had purchased. One Saturday, the homeless boy, his mother, and his siblings were asked by a church member to meet him at the vacant lot. They drove down the dirt road, which sloped into a cul-de-sac, expecting to see a parcel of weed-infested dirt. Instead, sitting proudly in its place, was their father's dream home. Cars dotted the shoulder all along the road, and people were walking around with shovels, hammers, paintbrushes, plants, and carpet.

"What's going on?" the boy asked. As he walked closer to the house, he saw all the activity of a giant anthill, with men busy painting the exterior, installing new windows, and planting bushes and trees. Inside the home was the enchanting smell of new carpet. Women were seemingly everywhere hanging curtains, arranging new furniture, and guiding movers as they installed appliances.

Puzzled and surprised by the day's events, the boy walked out the back door and around to the front, trying to digest what was happening. Standing some distance from the house, he stared at the workers and asked himself in utter disbelief, *Why are they doing this? Why are they helping my family? We can never pay them back.*

The volunteers' gift helped the boy recognize the value he had in God's eyes. The home also provided dignity and stability beyond description for the boy and his homeless family. The tragic death of a father and husband who had planned to build a dream home for his family was fulfilled by Christians who put feet to their faith and action to their convictions.

Some months later, the man who had originally sold the land to the family dropped by to pay his respects to the grieving widow. He had recently paved the road and planned to build other homes on the street. With a smile of deep satisfaction, he presented the woman a special gift in honor of her deceased husband. It was a wooden sign that would mark the name of the new street. When she read the sign her tears began to flow. The street would be named after her husband and my dad—Donaldson Court.

CHAPTER 9 IN REVIEW

Key Ideas

1. To Jesus, poverty is personal and relational.

2. Today, the most populous but hidden outcasts are the elderly, homeless families, and runaway youth.

3. Currently, 3.5 million Americans age sixty-five and older live below the poverty line.

4. Families with young children account for 50 percent of the nation's homeless population.

5. Twelve percent of the homeless population is made up of young people between the ages of sixteen and twenty-four.

Discussion Questions

1. Why was poverty personal and relational to Jesus? How personal and relational is it to you?

2. Who are the outcasts in your community? What is your church doing to meet their needs? What can you do to be a part of the solution?

3. Many senior adults live below the poverty line. What do you think is the solution to this growing problem?

4. Families are becoming homeless at an alarming rate. Sadly, many young children are caught up in unfortunate situations. Is the solution to this problem educational, governmental, spiritual, or a combination? Explain your response.

5. Why do you think so many young people are homeless? How do you respond when you encounter a homeless person? How does your reaction compare to what Jesus would have done?

DECLARE IT AND DO IT!

A Relentless life devoted to providing food for the hungry, water for the thirsty, shelter for the homeless, and offering tools for the poor to live a sustainable life may seem like an overwhelming task and so daunting it's hard to know where to start.

Experiments with people lost in a wilderness or in the desert almost always result in those people going in circles and returning to where they started. Similarly, the Relentless with all of their fervor and good intentions still need a compass or a road map for changing the world. So, here's how you can get started . . .

GO AHEAD AND DECLARE IT

Jesus announced at the very beginning of His ministry His priorities:

> The Spirit of the Lord is on me, because he has anointed me to preach good news to the poor. He has sent me to proclaim freedom for the prisoners and recovery of sight for

the blind, to release the oppressed, to proclaim the year of the Lord's favor.

—Luke 4:18–19, quoting Isaiah 61:1

Jesus publicly announced that the focus of His mission was the poor, the brokenhearted, and the captives. He unashamedly proclaimed that He would bring help for their earthly bodies and hope for their eternal souls. Jesus didn't fear failure or wait to be picked; He just declared it and did it. Then as His mission on earth was winding down (or should I say up), He emboldened His followers (including us) by claiming we would do greater things than He did (John 14:12). Think about it: more good news to the oppressed, and more people set free from the oppression of hunger, sickness, and injustice!

So what are you waiting for? Go ahead and declare your mission to your family and friends. In response to my challenge you might reply:

"I'm afraid because the declaration requires commitment and risk."

Let's face it. Our culture has brainwashed us into avoiding both because of the fear of failure and possible ridicule. A "No Failure Policy" is impossible and will straightjacket you from ever trying. Not starting is far worse than being wrong. If you start, at least you have the option of making adjustments to right the course. According to Jesus, you can't lose. He said we should not only declare what He declared but we should believe Him to accomplish even more!

"I will wait to declare it until I have accomplished _____."

The founders of America declared their independence from British tyranny on July 4, 1776, when they were losing the Revolutionary War and had been warned that their rebellion would result in their execution. At the time it did not make a lot of sense, but their Declaration of Independence and subsequent Constitution became the roadmap to success even amidst the most extreme challenges. The Relentless declare it in advance of their mission even when it is hard to define it or defend it.

"I'll wait until someone asks for my help and chooses me."

Listen, you are already chosen so why are you waiting to be picked? Sadly, even the most courageous can shrink from opportunity because they think they first have to be asked or hired.

One of my favorite movies is *It's A Wonderful Life*, with Jimmy Stewart. It is the story of George Bailey, who reluctantly inherits and manages his dad's bank but makes the most of it by helping many of his neighbors. After being falsely accused of a crime, he runs away and wishes that he had never been born. When George's wish is granted by the angel Clarence, he discovers what his community would have become without his influence. Everywhere George looks he sees his friends in despair. Their homes lost, businesses closed, and the spirit of community dashed because George was not there to help. George then realizes how much his life really mattered. It's a good thing for Bedford Falls that he didn't hide behind excuses or wait to be chosen before investing in the lives of his neighbors. Don't wait! Declare it because you matter to God and the people he has destined for you to help. They need your creativity, entrepreneurial ideas, and fearlessness.

"I'd like to, but I lack the resources to do it so why declare it?"

As discussed earlier, global transformation begins with personal transformation of our faith and priorities. If we are to follow in

Jesus' footsteps we must listen to His call for a radically different way of thinking about resources. This first includes how we prioritize the use or our own time, talents, and money. Instead of hoarding our wealth, Jesus challenges us to give it to those who need it most: "Sell your possessions and give to the poor" (Luke 12:33).

Secondy, we are challenged to look for assets in the world and link them to the needs: "If you spend yourselves in behalf of the hungry and satisfy the needs of the oppressed, then your light will rise in the darkness, and your night will become like the noonday. The LORD will guide you always; he will satisfy your needs in a sun-scorched land and will strengthen your frame. You will be like a well-watered garden, like a spring whose waters never fail" (Is. 58:10–11). You can declare it with a promise that God will not only meet your needs but you will become a spring of resources to the poor that will never run dry.

Following this chapter is "The Declarations to Join the Relentless Movement of Hope." I challenge you to get started by checking the boxes beside each declaration and determining when and how to declare your mission to family members and friends.

JUST DO IT

When someone asked Katie Davis why she had given up college scholarships, engagement to a fiancé, and a comfortable life in Tennessee to care for orphaned children in Africa, she replied: "This is the spot on the map where God has asked me to do the things I do—like pour out my heart for children who are hungry or alone, to try to help people leave harmful work and learn skills that will help them care for their families, or to assist women who are struggling to raise their children alone."[1] The point here is not to discourage someone from getting an education or becoming married. For many these are two of the most valuable assets in God's treasure chest for world changers. Yet, for the other "Katies" reading this, God is moving you out of the comfort of your home, your relationships, your office, your profession, your country in order to do it.

Everyone is not called like Katie to serve in a foreign land. Instead many of the Relentless can be found in their own Bedford Falls, volunteering at their church or a local charity, personally touching one person at a time. Mother Theresa said, "If you can't feed one hundred . . . then just feed one." She understood the liberation and life-giving power of serving others when nobody is paying you or forcing you to do it. You are simply doing it because you choose to do it.

THROW YOUR SHOE!

The pastor's face was drawn and worn as we stood in his parking lot gazing at the charred remains of his church building. The pastor confided, "Due to the lack of resources and growing threat of crime in this neighborhood we decided to move our church to a more secure location." His eyes filled with tears as he confided, "I knew we were running from our mission field, but I caved into the pressures of some of our church elders and key financial supporters." Becoming angrier with himself, the pastor continued, "And the decision to move out stirred such anger in the community and towards me personally that some of the gangs burned it down. This is all that is left."

I followed the pastor as he led me through the burnt rubble while pointing to different rooms of the church. It was a moving sight for me to see that this place where families had gathered each Sunday for worship and instruction was now nothing more than a pile of ashes. As we entered the nursery area, the pastor looked especially discouraged as we stood amidst ash-covered toys.

Feeling this man's hurt, I took off my shoe and threw it into the pile of burnt toys. The pastor looked at me as if the smoke inhalation was making me crazy. "What are you doing?" he exclaimed. "Pastor, in the book of Ruth we see that the shoe represented 'ownership' or 'taking authority over' (Ruth 4:6–7). Then years later King David proclaimed, 'Upon Edom I toss my sandal; over Philistia I shout in triumph. . . . Give us aid against the enemy, for the help of man is worthless. With God we will gain the victory, and he will trample down our enemies.'" (Ps. 60:8–12).

"I threw my shoe as a declaration that you as the leader are taking authority over this land and proclaiming today that this church is not moving out but moving in to take back what the enemy has stolen!" I glanced over at the pastor and with determined grit and tears streaming down his cheeks, he took off both his shoes and threw them into the pile of rubble!

Throughout this book, we have taken an honest look at some of the tragic problems that face our world. And this tragedy is not about abstractions—numbers and graphs and charts. It's about real, living human beings like you and me, people who are struggling against the odds, hoping to find a better life for their sons and daughters, and expending most of their energy just trying to survive. Many of them are fighting a losing battle. Millions in our world—adults and children alike—are without adequate food, without clean water, without even the most rudimentary health care, without housing and shelter, and without much hope for the future. At the same time, others throughout the world—and you and I are among them—have plenty. While some people have little or no food, we have full pantries and refrigerators. While some have to walk many miles to obtain a jug of clear water, all we have to do is turn the faucet. While children die of treatable diseases and adults go without much-needed medical attention, most of us have ready access to doctors who can deal with even our smallest physical complaints. And while countless people have either no shelter or one that is makeshift at best, we sit in the comfort of our homes.

{ *You feel the stirrings within your heart to stop turning a deaf ear or complaining and to actually do something to help.* }

As the Relentless, you look at the huge challenge of world poverty and natural disaster relief and instead of averting your eyes from the problems you see opportunity. You feel the stirrings within your heart to stop turning a deaf ear or complaining and to actually do something to help. The Relentless are joining forces with others who share similar passions and beliefs. Together we can make the world a better, safer, healthier, and hope-filled place. This relentless movement of hope is gaining force all around us, and it will not be stopped or even slowed.

Relentless, take off your shoe and throw it towards your home, neighborhood, job, or school! Throw your shoe towards the suffering and victims of injustice in your community, nation, and around the world! Throw your shoe as a declaration that you are going to continue Jesus' mission.

You are the Relentless. We have been waiting for. You give us hope!

CHAPTER 10 IN REVIEW

Key Ideas

1. Compassion is not optional for the believer.

2. The task of meeting the needs of the world will seem overwhelming unless you break it down into small steps.

3. If you are willing to be a world changer, God may move you out of your comfort zone.

4. You can make excuses or you can declare your decision.

5. Together the Relentless can make the world a better, safer, healthier, and hope-filled place.

Discussion Questions

1. Why is compassion not optional for believers? Have you ever felt it was optional for you? How have your feelings changed?

2. List some small steps you can take to change the life of someone in need.

3. Has God ever moved you out of your comfort zone? Describe how that affected your life.

4. Do you find yourself making excuses instead of making efforts to help the poor? What can you do to change that?

5. What do you think you can do to combat the issues discussed in the pages of this book?

The Declarations to Join
the Relentless Movement of Hope

———

A successful revolution has a clearly articulated reason for needing to overthrow the status quo. Thomas Jefferson, for example, penned the Declaration of Independence as a statement of what the American Revolution was all about. It contained the ideas, beliefs, and commitments that rallied people to the revolution, and it inspired those who had been content sitting on the sidelines to get personally involved.

Perhaps we, the Relentless, need a similar declaration of our goals, purposes, and commitments in the fight against poverty, sickness, disease, and economic injustice. We need to agree that to consign other human beings to living in squalor, need, and despair is unacceptable!

My own version of such a Declarations for the Relentless was introduced in Chapter 1. I offer it not as a definitive statement but as a starting point for the Relentless to think about the problems we face and how to begin taking action for real change.

I challenge you to check the boxes to the left of each declaration outlined below. Once you have carefully evaluated each one, join the movement of hope by signing your name and noting the date. This will serve as a reminder to you of the time when you declared that you were all in and were willing to become part of the force of change we call this relentless movement of hope.

☐ **I will sell sugar water and change the world.**

The Relentless, regardless of vocation, look for opportunities to share the good news in both word and deed to the poor, to proclaim freedom for victims of injustice, recovery of sight for the blind, to release the oppressed, to proclaim eternal hope found only by receiving and following Jesus Christ (Luke 4:18–19).

☐ I am committed to making the church more relevant and not abandoning it.

The Relentless are impassioned about helping the church pursue its potential through prayer, innovation, collaboration, and personally giving their time and resources to help the poor across the seas and across the street.

☐ I will offer the best help to the poor by bringing together people and solutions.

The Relentless are Kingdom-minded diplomats who build bridges across denominational and ethnic lines. They reach out to businesses, nonprofit organizations, and government agencies to bring together people and expertise in a movement of hope.

☐ I will humbly serve local leaders where they are needed most whether at home or in foreign countries.

The Relentless understand that many indigenous people—especially in third world countries—believe that visiting foreigners are well-meaning but are bent on taking over instead of learning their culture and serving where needed most. The Relentless will slip into the sandals of Jesus and follow His example of being a servant.

☐ I will hold charities accountable to the funds they raise for the poor.

The Relentless are not only generous in their giving but are impassioned about making sure people and organizations do what they say they are going to do for the poor.

☐ **I will do whatever it takes to defend the poor from injustice.**

The Relentless will protect and defend those who live in the margins. God protects those who cannot protect themselves by using Relentless followers who defend the rights of the vulnerable.

☐ **I will not assume that someone else will do it.**

The Relentless refuse to act as if someone else will do the job. They proactively look for opportunities to serve the least and the lost. The Relentless refuse to wear a "Do Not Disturb" sign because they believe that life is a series of divine appointments just waiting for them.

☐ **I am willing and eager to learn from the poor.**

The Relentless feel closest to God when they are with the poor because the poor are so close to the heart of God. The poor can teach us much, for example, how to be grateful instead of selfish. The poor also teach us a simple faith in God.

☐ **I will avoid compassion fatigue because I am plugged into an unlimited power source.**

The Relentless are plugged into God, the eternal source of wisdom, strength, joy, and compassion. Without Him to strengthen us, we cannot hope to keep ourselves focused and fueled to help others. We will quickly fall back on self-reliance, the desire for comfort, and the demand for short-term solutions.

☐ **I will go as far as you can see and then I will see farther.**

The Relentless understand the urgency of the hour and how many children and adults are fighting to survive because they lack adequate food, clean water, health care, and shelter. There is much the Relentless can do right now, but the Relentless also understand the importance of getting adequately prepared and growing spiritually, emotionally, physically, and educationally to become the most effective instruments God can use to offer healing and hope to the world. Serving the poor is a process of preparing the soil, sharpening our tools, planting the seed, and watering it. Over time the fruits of our labor become the seed for future opportunities to make a difference.

By signing my name below I will humbly submit myself to the Lord and His Relentless Movement of Hope.

_____   _____

Name   *Date*

About the Authors

Dave Donaldson is the cofounder of Convoy of Hope, an international organization providing disaster relief, building supply lines, sponsoring Health and Job Fairs, drilling wells, and supporting the Children's Feeding Initiative. Dave launched a global initiative for Convoy called Hope Experience, which enables business, government, and church leaders to spend one week in Africa, Israel, Asia, or South America experiencing the culture, and exploring ways to lift people out of poverty. Since its inception in 1994, Convoy of Hope has helped over 50 million people worldwide.

Dave Donaldson has addressed leaders around the world on the role of faith in community. He has been a guest on numerous Christian and secular television and radio programs and has authored several books. Dave earned his Master's Degree in Intercultural Studies from Fuller Theological Seminary in Pasadena, California, focusing on "Developing and implementing social programs in a cross-cultural environment."

Donaldson is also President of Charity Awards International www.charityawards.com, which celebrates the outstanding examples of public and private figures who devote themselves to working for others. Since its inception in 1980, The International Charity Awards has had various Presidents and First Ladies serve as chairpersons and has raised millions of dollars for philanthropic causes.

He has coordinated White House briefings, roundtables, and conference calls between community and government leaders. In 2003, Dave was appointed by former Secretary of Health and Human

Services Tommy Thompson to serve on his National Council for Mental Health and Substance Abuse and to chair the Faith-based Committee. He hosted an historic summit for foster care and adoption with the US Children's Bureau. He serves on several boards, including the National Courage Awards, which honors NFL players who have shown courage on and off the field.

Dave, his wife, Kristy, and their four children reside in the Springfield, Missouri, area.

Terry Glaspey is the author of a dozen books, including *Not a Tame Lion: The Spiritual Legacy of C. S. Lewis*; *25 Keys to Life-Changing Prayer*; and the best-selling *Bible Basics for Everyone*. He is an author, speaker, compassion advocate, and works in the publishing industry.

About Convoy of Hope

Since Convoy of Hope, a 501(c)3 faith-based nonprofit, was founded in 1994 we have served more than 50 million people throughout the world through international children's feeding initiatives, community outreaches, disaster responses, and partner resourcing.

Currently, there are more than 100,000 children in our feeding initiatives in El Salvador, Haiti, Dominican Republic, Honduras, Kenya, Nicaragua, and the Philippines. Through the feeding initiatives children and their families receive good nutrition, clean and safe drinking water, instruction on agricultural techniques, healthy living environments, and an opportunity for an education.

Year after year, Convoy of Hope is lauded for its effectiveness and efficiency in mobilizing tens of thousands of volunteers for community outreaches and disaster responses.

No matter what Convoy of Hope is doing, its constant objective is to deliver much-needed food, supplies, and hope to the impoverished and suffering.

Learn more about Convoy of Hope by visiting
www.convoyofhope.com.

Notes

Chapter One

1. Bob Goff, *Love Does: Discover a Secretly Incredible Life in an Ordinary World* (Nashville, TN: Thomas Nelson, 2012).
2. Katie J. Davis, *Kisses from Katie: A Story of Relentless Love and Devotion* (Nashville, TN: Howard Books, 2011).
3. http://www.convoyofhope.org/go/headlines/entry/when_life_hands_you_lemons/
4. Bill Hybels, *Courageous Leadership* (Grand Rapids, MI: Zondervan, 2002), 23.
5. http://my.ilstu.edu/~jabraun/students/geiseman/facts.htm
6. As quoted in Dave Donaldson and Terry Glaspey, *The Compassion Revolution: How God Can Use You to Meet the World's Greatest Needs* (Eugene, Or.: Harvest House Publishers, 2010), 52.
7. http://www.infowars.com/articles/us/katrina_no_red_cross.htm
8. UNICEF, The State of the World's Children 2009, 133.
9. http://www2.ohchr.org/english/bodies/hrcouncil/docs/17session/A.HRC.17.46.pdf
10. UNICEF, The State of the World's Children 2007: Women and Children; The Double Dividend of Gender Equality, 5, http://www.unicef.org/sowc07/docs/sowc07.pdf.
11. http://www.childinfo.org/protection.html
12. Malcolm Gladwell, *The Tipping Point: How Little Things Can Make a Big Difference* (Boston, MA: Back Bay Books, 2002), 28.
13. http://www.writespirit.net/authors/mother-teresa/mother-teresa-quotes/teresa-jesus/
14. Richard Stearns, *The Hole in Our Gospel* (Nashville, TN: Thomas Nelson, Inc., 2009), 238.
15. Carmine Gallo, *The Innovative Secrets of Steve Jobs: Insanely Different Principles for Breakthrough Success* (McGraw Hill; New York, 2010), 108.

Chapter Two

1. Donald P. McNeill, Douglas A. Morrison, and Henri J. M. Nouwen, *Compassion: A Reflection on the Christian Life* (New York: Doubleday, 1982), 25.

Chapter Three

1. http://topdocumentaryfilms.com/super-size-me/
2. http://www.strategicstoragetrust.com/self-storage-industry/key-facts.aspx

3. Ibid.

4. http://en.wikipedia.org/wiki/Enron_scandal

5. http://en.wikipedia.org/wiki/Enron:_The_Smartest_Guys_in_the_Room

6. http://topics.nytimes.com/top/reference/timestopics/subjects/f/foreclosures/index.html

7. http://www.npr.org/2011/06/04/136930966/how-much-is-14-3-trillion-it-s-a-brain-tease

8. http://www.nationalreview.com/corner/265466/dont-raise-debt-ceiling-andrew-c-mccarthy#

Chapter Four

1. http://themoreheadnews.com/fridayspost/x744033547/More-than-the-richest-man-in-the-cemetery

2. http://philanthroplist.com/bill-gates-philanthropist/

3. http://www.evangelicalsforsocialaction.org/document.doc?id=113

4. http://www.usnews.com/opinion/blogs/economic-intelligence/2012/03/08/helping-the-super-rich-at-the-expense-of-the-super-poor

5. Ronald J. Sider, *Rich Christians in an Age of Hunger: Moving from Affluence to Generosity* (Nashville, TN: Thomas Nelson, Inc., 2005), xiv.

6. http://www.gatesfoundation.org/about/pages/bill-melinda-gates-letter.aspx

7. http://www.gatesfoundation.org/annual-letter/2012/Pages/home-en.aspx

8. As quoted in Dave Donaldson and Terry Glaspey, *The Compassion Revolution*, 158.

9. http://www.ccfmm.com/index.php?option=com_content&view=article&id=20:stewardship-quotes&catid=8:grant-information&Itemid=11

Chapter Five

1. http://www.nrlc.org/Factsheets/FS03_AbortionInTheUS.pdf

2. http://www.ehow.com/how_12117589_hold-up-stretching-plants.html

3. Preached by Tommy Barnett at his Pastors' School, Phoenix, AZ, 1991.

Chapter Six

1. http://www.buzzle.com/articles/facts-on-world-hunger.html

2. http://www.childinfo.org/undernutrition.html

3. These are my own calculations based on 210,000 dying each week from water-related diseases.

4. Randy Alcorn, *Managing God's Money: A Biblical Guide* (Carol Stream, IL: Tyndale House, 2011), 144.

5. As quoted in Donaldson and Glaspey, *The Compassion Revolution*, 76.

6. http://www.bread.org/hunger/us/

7. Richard Stearns, *The Hole in Our Gospel* (Nashville, TN: Thomas Nelson, Inc., 2009), 135.

8. http://www.rt.com/news/usa-food-waste-hungry-345/; http://www.foodnavigator
-usa.com/Business/US-wastes-half-its-food

9. http://www.wstar.org/windstar/Education/LivingLightly/worldhunger.html

10. http://en.wikipedia.org/wiki/2010_Haiti_earthquake

Chapter Seven

1. http://www.childinfo.org/water.html

2. UN Water, Tackling a Global Crisis: International Year of Sanitation 2008;
http://esa.un.org/iys/docs/IYS_flagship_web_small.pdf

3. http://tlc.howstuffworks.com/home/25-things-might-not-know-water.htm

4. http://www.wutc.wa.gov/webimage.nsf/3183343b012337b48825669b0077676f
/38333ff6130fc26988256959007655ef!opendocument

5. http://blueplanetnetwork.org/water/facts

6. http://www.water.cc/water-crisis/water-and-education/

7. http://blueplanetnetwork.org/water/facts

8. http://www.genderhealth.org/files/uploads/change/change_in_the_media/CQ
_Researcher_6_11.pdf

9. http://www.facebook.com/note.php?note_id=178607972188454

10. Ibid.

Chapter Eight

1. http://www.childinfo.org/fgmc.html

2. http://www.childinfo.org/files/ChildProtection__from_violence_exploitation
_abuse.pdf

3. http://www.aacap.org/cs/root/facts_for_families/foster_care

Chapter Nine

1. http://www.aoa.gov/aoaroot/aging_statistics/Profile/2011/docs/2011profile.pdf

2. http://www.nationalhomeless.org/factsheets/families.html

3. http://www.endhomelessness.org/content/article/detail/4361

4. www.endhomelessness.org/files/1224_file_FamiliesFMac.pdf

5. Piers Morgan Tonight, CNN, Interview with Mark Wahlberg, January 13, 2012.

6. http://american-business.org/3210-rowland-h-macy-1822-1877.html

7. George Barna, *Grow Your Church from the Outside In: Understanding the
Unchurched and How to Reach Them* (Ventura, CA.: Regal Books, 2004), 114.

Chapter Ten

1. Davis, *Kisses from Katie:*, 12.

TO ORDER MORE COPIES

visit www.influenceresources.com